WHO IS GOD?

Examining His Character From A to Z

By
Barbara Ann Kay

TEACH Services, Inc.
P U B L I S H I N G
www.TEACHServices.com

Copyright revised © 2011 Barbara Ann Kay and TEACH Services, Inc.
ISBN-13: 978-1-57258-958-2 (Paperback)
ISBN-13: 978-1-57258-959-9 (E-Book)
Library of Congress Control Number: 2011942221

Previously titled
God's Character From A to Z

Published by

TEACH Services, Inc.

P U B L I S H I N G

www.TEACHServices.com

CONTENTS

PREFACE

For fifty years I've been on a spiritual journey. Raised in a Christian home, I came to know Jesus as a personal Friend at an early age. I embraced Him as my loving Savior during my childhood, although for some years I felt uncertain about my salvation. I sought answers from God about difficult stuff life threw my way. I questioned how He is good yet allows bad things to happen. I've wondered what God is really like.

Along the pathway on which God walks with me, I've experienced His touch in my life, heard His voice whispering to my heart, and have come to know that His love is enough. In His Word, the Bible, I've been discovering gems of truth about God's character that have blessed me.

This book is some of what God has shown me regarding Himself. He is the Alpha and the Omega, the Beginning and the End, the First and the Last (Revelation 1:8, 11, 17). Rather than using the Greek alphabet starting with Alpha, I've taken each letter of the English alphabet, and beginning with A, I have attempted to portray the vastness and beauty of God's character. This book is not a theological presentation of God. I have merely sat at my Lord's feet and asked Him, "Show me Your glory."

It is my prayer that while reading the pages of this book your appetite will be whetted to know God better. "And this is eternal life, that they might know You, the only true God, and Jesus Christ whom You have sent." (John 17:3)

Chapter 1
ALMIGHTY GOD

"He who dwells in the secret place of the Most High shall abide under the shadow of the Almighty." (Psalm 91:1)

When my heart is heavy, I like to stroll outside at night with my head tilted skyward. Gazing at the myriads of stars sprinkled across the heavens gives me a fresh perspective of my situation. I am awed by the creative power of the Almighty God of the universe. I think, *since God made all those stars, He is able to take care of everything concerning me. Yet, how can such a God be interested in little me?* Perhaps David felt this way when he wrote, "What is man that You take thought of him, And the son of man that You care for him?" (Psalm 8:4 [NASB])

Some people suggest that God created this planet and then abandoned man to his fate. Others question, "If God is so strong and mighty, why doesn't He do something about all the tragedy in this world?" It seems hard to trust an Almighty God when our world seems out of control. While it is humanly impossible to explain the workings of the Almighty God, or lack of His intervention, one must remember how reassuring it is to serve a powerful God "who is able to do exceedingly abundantly above all that we ask or think." (Ephesians 3:20) The question remains, why doesn't He?

One November afternoon in 1980, the phone rang. I set my 10-month-old daughter on the floor and stepped across the room to answer it. Immediately, I knew something was wrong. It was my mother's voice, and this was the first time she had ever called me from Chiapas, Mexico. Her words both shocked me and broke my heart. "Your daddy is dead. His airplane went down in the jungle, and everyone on board was killed." My mother gave me a list of names to call, including his mother.

After assuring Mom that my brothers and I would come as soon as possible, I hung up the phone and burst into deep sobs. How could this terrible thing have happened? My daddy was a mission pilot helping many people. Two pastors died with him, for they were flying to a village for a baptism. Why hadn't God protected them? It was a terrible day as I told my brothers and grandparents the awful news. We found no answers to our deep pain and loss.

For many years I continued asking my Almighty God, "Why?" One afternoon He whispered to my heart, "Just trust Me even though you don't understand. I have a plan. You will see your daddy again when I raise him from his grave. Together you will live with Me in heaven."

Another November afternoon, this time in 1999, the phone rang. Two weeks earlier my daughter had given birth prematurely to a tiny baby girl. All the young parents could do was to stand by their baby's incubator in the Neonatal Intensive Care Unit and pray for the life of their child. They were on their way to the hospital now.

With dread I answered the phone. It was one of the NICU doctors. "I'm sorry, but we've done everything we can for your granddaughter. She's not going to make it." I told him her parents would be there any minute, and then I fell on my knees before my Almighty God and pleaded for Him to stretch out His hand and touch Michaela.

How could I give up another family member this week of Thanksgiving? Seeing my daughter and son grieving wrenched my heart. I struggled but continued to pray, "Not my will, but Yours be done."

It was a miracle Michaela had lived at birth, being only twenty-four weeks old. Her skin was transparent and her eyes still sealed shut. Every modern technology was employed to save her life, but infections had invaded her tiny body and toxins were building because her kidneys had shut down. She wasn't responding to the medicine, and sadly, the doctors could give no hope.

After Michaela's birth my Bible would fall open at this passage every morning. "Ah, LORD GOD! behold, thou hast made the heaven and the earth by Thy great power and stretched out arm, and there is nothing too hard for Thee." (Jeremiah 32:17 [KJV]) I clung to this promise.

The phone call came on Friday. All day Sabbath we prayed, spending hours outside the door where our precious baby lay. Early Sunday morning Elders met with our family to pray and anoint Michaela, asking God for healing. The nurses let my children hold their baby for the first time, thinking it would be the last. There was no change in her condition, but we clung to hope, trusting that with God nothing is impossible. The next morning Michaela's nurse called to report that she had peed a little, and soon blood tests revealed that toxin levels were decreasing. A miracle! I cannot explain why sometimes God protects and heals while sometimes He doesn't. However, I know that there is nothing too hard for the Lord. We may not understand the ways of our God, but we can trust Him.

Consider Abraham. In obedience to God's call, Abram left his hometown to travel to a distant country. He and Sarai lived in a tent as pilgrims and strangers in Canaan. One night God met with Abram under the stars. God told him, "Look at all the stars and count them, if you can. Your descendants will be just as many." That night God made Abram a two-fold promise—a son and land. Since his wife was barren, Abram wondered how this would happen, but he believed God.

Abram waited for years for God to fulfill His promise but caved in at Sarai's suggestion to take her maidservant as a second wife. In those days this was a legal way to bear a son to carry on the family name. Abram thought, *maybe this is God's way of providing an heir.* Abram and Sarai found out it wasn't. Their decision to take things into their own hands, rather than trusting God's ability to fulfill what He'd promised, only resulted in grief.

Even though God is almighty, He sets limits on what He'll do. To His created beings God has given the freedom to make decisions. God allows us, as He did Abram, to choose and then bear the consequences of those choices. Because we fail to trust God's timing, not allowing Him to fulfill His plan for our lives, He often has to resort to plan B, C, D, or even Z. God says that with Him nothing is impossible, even creating babies in barren wombs. Yet, when years pass without our seeing the Almighty God at work, even those strong in faith may wonder and waver.

When Abram was ninety-nine years old God appeared to him saying, "I am Almighty God; walk before Me and be blameless. And I will make My covenant between Me and you, and will multiply you exceedingly... You shall be a father of many nations." (Genesis 17:1, 4) God changed his name to Abraham, which means father of a great multitude, and gave his wife the name Sarah, meaning princess. Sarah was now ninety years of age; she was not only barren but well past the child-bearing years. Now was God's time, and Isaac, which means laughter, was born to Abraham and Sarah.

With God nothing is impossible. He can bring laughter into our lives. We must never give up!

When Isaac was a young man, God tested Abraham. "Take now your son, your only son Isaac, whom you love, and go to the land of Moriah, and offer him there as a burnt offering on one of the mountains of which I shall tell you." (Genesis 22:2) Abraham wondered, *how could God be asking for a human sacrifice, such as the heathen offer, contrary to His express command? If I kill my son, how will God fulfill His promise?*

With a heavy heart Abraham made the three-day journey, Isaac walking by his side. Constantly praying for strength to do God's will, impossible though it seemed, Abraham fought off Satan's temptations to doubt. To Isaac's question, "Where is the lamb for a burnt offering?" Abraham answered, "God will provide for Himself the lamb." (Genesis 22:8)

God did. As Abraham raised the knife to slay his beloved son, the voice of the Angel of the LORD stopped him. Abraham noticed a ram caught in a nearby thicket, and together he and Isaac offered it as a burnt offering. Abraham passed the test, and before the watching universe a symbolic picture of God sacrificing His Son was displayed.

Through the descendants of Abraham, God sent His only begotten Son in human flesh to be the Savior of the world. Almighty God committed the reputation of His character to His beloved Son and the work of making the fulfillment of His promises to Abraham possible. Paul writes, "You are all one in Christ Jesus, and if you are Christ's, then you are Abraham's seed, and heirs according to the promise." (Galatians 3:28, 29)

Before the creation of the world, Father and Son had covenanted together to save man, even at the risk of eternal loss and failure. Stand at the cross and behold the almighty hand of God clasped to His side while His Son suffers and dies to pay the wages of sin. Before the cross, Jesus had prayed, "Oh Father, if it is possible, let this cup pass from Me!" However, Jesus submitted to fulfilling salvation's plan by bearing the sins of the world upon the cross. Feeling forsaken and separated from God, He died of a broken heart. At Calvary no voice stayed the knife that pierced the heart of Jesus. God had provided Himself a Lamb.

One day in heaven God will explain His working, and we will acknowledge that His ways are perfect. The redeemed will sing an anthem of praise. "Great and marvelous are Your works, Lord God Almighty! Just and true are Your ways, O King of the saints! Who shall not fear You, O Lord, and glorify Your name? For You alone are holy. For all nations shall come and worship before You, for Your judgments are made manifest." (Revelation 15:3, 4 [KJV])

Chapter 2

GOD OF ALL BLESSINGS

"Blessed be the God and Father of our Lord Jesus Christ, who has blessed us with every spiritual blessing in the heavenly places in Christ." (Ephesians 1:3)

I've been asked, "How do you know God is good?" God's character is being scrutinized by millions of His created children based on what they see happening on this earth. Many conditions and catastrophes are constructed by the devil, but the suffering and pain which result are attributed to God.

When I consider the character of God, the first thing that comes to mind is all that He does for me. He loves me so much, pouring out blessings until I am the richest, happiest person alive! I don't always feel this way, nor act like it, but when I think about all God has done for me and my family, I feel truly blessed. God is the source of every wonderful blessing, and He sends His gifts in various packages. He delights in surprising His children.

So many of God's blessings I take for granted, such as being able to see: tiny lavender violets nestled in the grass; a bright red cardinal flitting through the air; puffy white clouds scattered across a deep blue sky; a brilliant sunset of orange and purple shades; a child's smile. Also, I forget the blessing of hearing: a creek bubbling over rocks; bird songs; laughter; a friend's voice; music melodies. Then there's the sense of smell: fresh baked bread, or a simmering kettle of vegetable stew; clean laundry and shampooed hair; freshly mown grass; summer rain; crisp autumn air. Oh, the delights of taste: juicy grapes, oranges, and peaches; creamy avocadoes; luscious berries; all kinds of crunchy nuts; a drink of cool spring water. What if I couldn't feel? Couldn't feel warm sunshine on my face; cool breezes; hugs given me by family and friends; a hot shower massaging my tired back muscles; a soft, warm comforter pulled up to my neck; the soft fur of my bunny as I pet him. With a heart of gratitude I can say, "Blessed be the Lord, who daily loadeth us with benefits, even the God of our salvation." (Psalm 68:19 [KJV])

During my life I've accumulated in my blessing basket a wide variety of gifts from my Father. Let me share a few.

The assurance of salvation I claim among my most treasured blessings. Although I grew up a Christian, I thought for many years that I had to do something to earn my salvation. I struggled with becoming perfect and not succeeding even for a day. I battled a temper that, no matter how hard I tried, I could not conqueror. My patience was forever running out in dealing with my children. One day I gave up, and falling on my knees, I told Jesus, "You can have me just as I am and make me whatever You wish, but I cannot overcome, and I'm tired of trying." God's blessing of peace entered my soul, and since that day I know I am secure in my Father's hands.

Another spiritual blessing is God adopting me as His child. I have a Father and a place to belong. He cradles me in His strong arms next to His heart. He provides for my every need and delivers me from my fears, replacing them with His joy. I am never alone because His Spirit dwells in me, and one day I'll live at His house. I am eternally loved.

Each day, as I commune with my Father God and Jesus my Savior, I receive blessings of consolation, instruction, correction, and encouragement. As I read God's Word, He whispers messages just for me, which makes me feel so special. It's a wonderful feeling to know I am understood when I pour out my thoughts into my Father's ears. God says, "I dwell in the high and holy place, with him who has a contrite and humble spirit." (Isaiah 57:15) I am overwhelmed with awe at a God who lives in me by His Spirit and is active in my life. What a blessing is my fellowship with Jesus!

Every Sabbath day is a blessing for me. To think that God wants me to spend a whole day just with Him romances my heart. Through the years I've experienced a double portion of spiritual blessings on His holy day. Attending worship services at my church is a habit with me, and often I am blessed by something that is shared.

However, the greatest Sabbath blessings I've received are out of doors in nature. One spring Sabbath my husband and I packed a picnic lunch, put on our hiking shoes, and drove to a mountain for the afternoon. The Lord quieted my soul as I strolled along a flower strewn pathway. I saw God's greatness in the huge trees we found in the woods. For hours I basked in the breeze and the freshness of spring green. My spirit was revived. Other Sabbaths I have hiked beside a bubbling stream, pausing awhile to soak my feet in the cool water. I've sat in a grove of pines in Mississippi, on a beach by the Atlantic Ocean in Mexico, and overlooking a lake in Tennessee, meditating on God's love and enjoying the fellowship of my Creator.

Many people have blessed my life, but none more than my husband. When I was ten years old, I began praying that God would lead me to the man I was to marry. I wanted Him to pick out my husband. At the time of my prayer, our family was living in southern Mexico at a mission institution.

When I was fifteen years old, my family traveled to Alabama to spend the summer with my aunt and uncle, who had informed us that teens could find work in the flower fields there. While my daddy was gone to Alaska, where he did commercial fishing each summer to provide for our support in the mission field, my mother and I were hired by a Christian couple to cut flowers. In the flower fields of Alabama, a girl from the *far* south met a boy from Sand Mountain. While I felt attracted to this handsome, hard working young man, I didn't know he was the one God had in mind for my future husband.

However, after spending several summers working together in the fields, he asked me one day after work, "Will you be my wife?" Someday I'd like to hear how God arranged all the details to get my family from the Northwest, where I was born and most our relatives live, to Alabama.

The day I became a mother the blessings of having children began to flow. God enriched my life with every precious bundle of joy. The companionship of my children—as toddlers, teens, and now adults—is a blessing I thank God for. With their marriages and the births of grandchildren, the fountain of family blessings increases.

Another blessing for me was being able to stay home with our children and home school them. God helped us stretch my husband's paycheck to meet all our needs. After the birth of our third child, God inspired Irdene to create a home business in conjunction with homeschooling. We began Pine Grove Nursery with shrubs and blueberry bushes.

Our nursery provided work opportunities for our children and a job for me at our front door. The extra money from the nursery sales helped meet the needs of our growing family.

One day my husband was offered a greenhouse frame, heaters, and fans just for disassembling and hauling them away. In time we switched from growing shrubs to propagating English ivy, which he sells wholesale to florists and garden centers. As our business grew Irdene eventually constructed four greenhouses. We have grown our business without going into debt, and God has blessed our efforts in a financial way. As our children have attended Christian academies and colleges, God has met the additional expense. I stand in awe at what He does to provide!

God has enriched my life with friendships. Some are for a season; others stick for a lifetime. After I began attending women's retreats, my circle of friends grew. These are my sisters in Christ with whom I stay in touch with via e-mail. I treasure the blessing of girlfriends.

When I was twelve years old, a family with five children came to the mission where we lived. The middle child, Toni, was ten years old. From the first afternoon we played together, she and I became best friends. We went to school together, played together with our brothers, and sometimes had sleepovers at each others houses. On Sabbath afternoons we went walking together. In fact, we did almost everything together. We even made a treasure box, which we hid in the woods between our houses. It was delightful to find little gifts and notes from each other in our special box.

When our families separated, each going to a different mission station, we missed each other. Toni and I stayed in touch for several years by mail, but we became busy with school and our own families so our letters dwindled to Christmas catch-ups. However, over the past several years, we are again sharing our lives via e-mail, sometimes even reminiscing about our childhood days.

When my youngest daughter was in sixth grade, I took her and several other girls to outdoor school at a camp. There I met Nell, who shared our cabin with the girls she had brought. In those three days she and I started talking, and we've never stopped! God gave me Nell to share life with during the days of midlife changes. We talk on the phone at least once a week and have shared many prayer requests, joyful experiences, and tearful concerns. Our friendship has blessed my life, even though we rarely can get together.

Yes, I have so much for which to be thankful. I feel so blessed. God is a loving God, and His sharing hand extends to all. He doesn't reserve blessings just for those who acknowledge His care. "He makes His sun rise on the evil and on the good, and sends rain on the just and on the unjust." (Matthew 5:45)

"Every good gift and every perfect gift is from above, and comes down from the Father of lights, with whom there is no variation or shadow of turning." (James 1:17)

God delights to give! He desires to lavish His blessings on you! I invite you to taste and see that God is good, and then relate to others what He has done for you.

Chapter 3

COMPASSIONATE COMFORTER WHO CARES

"Blessed be the God and Father of our Lord Jesus Christ, the Father of mercies and God of all comfort, who comforts us in all our tribulation, that we may be able to comfort those who are in any trouble, with the comfort with which we ourselves are comforted by God." (2 Corinthians 1:3, 4)

Maria sank into the chair and, burying her face in her hands, she let the tears come. Grief tore at her heart. Today she'd laid her little son in the grave. She and her husband had earnestly prayed that God would heal his sick body, but he had worsened and soon died. Her family mocked them, "It is because you joined that strange religion that your child died." She did not understand, but in this great sorrow, Maria clung to God's promises.

"Oh, Father God, comfort me. Help me be strong in my faith even though our family doesn't accept our new way of life. Bring some good out of our loss." Maria continued to pour out her heart into the ears of a compassionate God whom she'd come to love and serve. The hour grew late. Her older children slept. Even her husband had gone to bed.

Suddenly the darkened room became light as an angelic being appeared beside Maria. "God loves you. He cares about you. He has sent me to tell you that the child you now carry in your womb will be another boy." In wonder Maria listened to this personal message from God. The soothing words from heaven filled her heart with warmth and comfort. Slowly the light faded and darkness settled again in her humble home, but the darkness of her soul had been lifted. Maria knew that no matter what personal loss she suffered she would continue to lift up Jesus to her friends and family in the village where she and her husband lived.

When Jesus lived on this earth, He demonstrated what God is

like. In the gospels we can read about the people whose lives He touched. One of these was a widow who lived in Nain. Upon entering this village, Jesus met a funeral procession heading for the cemetery. Knowing this widow's dead son was her only means of support, He had compassion on her. "Weep not," Jesus said gently. Then He walked up to the open coffin and touched it. Commandingly, He said, "Young man, arise." The man sat up, and Jesus presented him to his mother.

You say, these are wonderful stories, but I've never had an angel bring me a message from God, nor have I experienced a resurrection miracle such as the widow of Nain did. We question, "If God is compassionate, why does He allow so much suffering?" Perhaps one reason God allows the difficult experiences of loss and pain is so we can empathize with others, sharing with them how God has been our Comforter.

One of my favorite declarations of God's love was written by the prophet Jeremiah at a difficult time in the history of his people. "Through the Lord's mercies we are not consumed, because His compassions fail not. They are new every morning. Great is Your faithfulness." (Lamentations 3:22, 23)

I love the picture of God as a compassionate and caring Shepherd. Jesus talks about Himself as the good Shepherd who knows His sheep and calls them all by name. Each of us is as fully known to our Shepherd as if we were the only one. He cares for us individually, meeting our spiritual needs as well as providing for our physical wants.

Our Shepherd leads us to places where we can eat, drink, and rest. Through dark valleys, where death seems certain, our Shepherd is with us. Amid trials and temptations, the good Shepherd embraces us to comfort and console. Because of His caring character, our Shepherd searches for His sheep who have wandered away from His side. When Jesus finds the lost sheep He carries it home, not with reprimands and punishment but with a song of rejoicing and tender words of comfort. Further, because Jesus cares more about the sheep than Himself, He willingly gave His life for us. (John 10)

I've experienced loss and pain during my life and made it through only because my compassionate and caring God was with me. He is my Comforter.

I clearly remember the day I miscarried our second baby. The bleeding would not abate, and preparations for an emergency D&C surgery were underway. I feared going under anesthesia. My husband had gone home at my request to get me some clothes and personal items since I'd have to remain in the hospital overnight. I felt so alone and very sad. Silently, I cried out to God, and He whispered to my heart, *cast all your care upon Me because I care about you* (1 Peter 5:7).

I gave Him my longing for a baby, my fears and tears, and He gave me peace and the assurance He was with me. The following year I gave birth to a healthy son. As I held my baby boy, I knew God truly cared.

Not merely in the valleys of the shadow of death where the enemy lurks have I experienced the caring nature of my Father, but in the ordinary things of everyday life.

When I was a teen the guys would let their girlfriends wear their watches when they were going steady—that's the term we used in the 70s. I'd been going out with my special guy for a couple years, but he didn't see any reason to part with his watch to carry out some tradition. However, I thought it would be special to wear his watch, even for a few days. When I expressed my desire, he reluctantly entrusted me with his watch, pocketing mine so he would know what time it was. I was happy wearing his watch, for this symbol upon my wrist declared to the world that I was chosen. I'd been wearing his watch for some time when one day I noticed that it had stopped. What was I going to do? He could not afford to buy another, and since the watch was in my possession, I felt responsible. Sitting among the trees, I talked to my caring God about this concern. "Please God," I begged. "Make this watch run again."

God did! The following day my boyfriend's watch was ticking away and keeping time. I returned it, thanking him for letting me wear it for awhile, and I thanked my God for caring about not only a watch but my feelings and our dating relationship. My boyfriend's watch was still running a year and a half later when I married him.

Whether my concerns are large or small, the Lord wants me to give every one to Him. With such a loving, caring God I wonder, *why do I so often forget to cast my burden upon the Lord and let Him sustain me?* (Psalm 55:22).

It was one of those days when I was feeling discouraged, alone, and overwhelmed. My children were occupied with their school lessons, so I pulled my chair next to the wood stove and opened a book on the life of Christ. Hungering for words of comfort and encouragement, I opened the pages in the middle of the book and began reading. "Every soul is as fully known to Jesus as if he were the only one for whom the Saviour died. The distress of every one touches His heart. The cry for aid reaches His ear … He cares for each one as if there were not another on the face of the earth … The soul that has given himself to Christ is more precious in His sight than the whole world. The Saviour would have passed through the agony of Calvary that one might be saved in His kingdom … Unless His followers choose to leave Him, He will hold them fast." (Ellen G. White, *The Desire of Ages*, p. 480)

What assuring words! I continued reading, knowing it wasn't by accident that I'd opened to this page. "Through all our trials we have a never-failing Helper. He does not leave us alone to struggle with temptation, to battle with evil, and be finally crushed with burdens and sorrow. Though now He is hidden from mortal sight, the ear of faith can hear His voice saying, Fear not; I am with you … I have endured your sorrows, experienced your struggles, encountered your temptations. I know your tears; I also have wept. The griefs that lie too deep to be breathed into any human ear, I know. Think not that you are desolate and forsaken. Though your pain touches no responsive chord in any heart on earth, look unto Me, and live." (Ellen G. White, *The Desire of Ages*, p. 483)

Tears filled my eyes as I felt God's presence. God's message to my heart that day is one I read when the enemy tells me lies. The truth about God is that He does care. I am not alone! He understands my trials and tears! He is my compassionate Savior who loves me beyond measure! He is the God of all comfort!

Chapter 4
CREATIVE DESIGNER

"For thus saith the LORD that created the heavens; God himself that formed the earth and made it; he hath established it; he created it not in vain, he formed it to be inhabited: I am the LORD, and there is none else." (Isaiah 45:18 [KJV])

In the Bible I read about a God who is the Master Designer of a city, a place Abraham and his descendents will one day dwell. (Hebrews 11:10) God is the Creator of everything in heaven and earth. (Isaiah 42:5; Colossians 1:16) In the universe there are many things which God has created; wonderful sights we can't even imagine. Beyond our solar system, in the vastness of eternal space, the Creator has designed worlds of beauty. One day when my feet are not bound to the soil of this earth, I plan to explore and enjoy the perfect creations of my God.

Even in this world marred by sin, I see evidences of God's creative design. What I enjoy most about spring are the flowers. To walk along a forest trail lined with wild blooms of trilliums, violets, creamy white anemones, deep purple delphiniums, bright yellow trout lilies, and purple phlox thrills my heart. Every flower is exquisitely unique. Whether I gaze upon orchids growing high in the trees, bury my nose in a wild rose bloom, or stoop to examine a clump of tiny bluets, I am awed by the rich beauty of a single flower.

When our children were small, we used to vacation at a Florida state park. We pitched our tent on the sand, strung a tarp over a table, and enjoyed the ocean. My favorite activity at the beach was hunting for shells. One evening as the sun was setting over the ocean and the tide was receding, we waded in waist deep water digging for shells with our feet. We found all sorts of treasures: curled shells with pink centers; long, pointed ones with brown markings; pink, yellow, and white scalloped ones. In the dusk we trudged along the shore with several bags of shells. At camp we washed our collection and packed them to bring home. Each shell shows that a Designer exists and that He enjoys variety.

I never cease to feel awed when I look into a night sky filled with stars. I have stood under a tropical sky where the stars appeared to hang so low that if I climbed a ladder I could touch them. I have felt close to my Creator when on a frigid evening I've stood in my yard gazing at millions of glittering stars. To view unmarred beauty one simply must "lift up your eyes on high, and behold who hath created these things, that bringeth out their host by number: He calleth them all by names by the greatness of His might, for that He is strong in power; not one faileth." (Isaiah 40:26 [KJV])

Whether visiting a zoo, walking through a fish aquarium exhibit, or strolling through a mountain park, one can see the creations of the Master Designer. However, what catches my eye above all is His crowning creation. Just yesterday in a store isle, I met a mother pushing a stroller with two babies. As I continued grocery shopping, I marveled at God's artwork in those precious lives. Everywhere I go I enjoy seeing babies and find joy in looking at their innocent little faces.

Our creative God has designed every person with unique features, personality, and abilities. David testified, "You formed my inward parts; You covered me in my mother's womb. I will praise You for I am fearfully and wonderfully made; Marvelous are Your works. . .My frame was not hidden from You, When I was made in secret, and skillfully wrought in the lowest parts of the earth." (Psalm 139:13-15)

Besides the creative works we see in nature, from the tall redwoods to the tiny hummingbirds, God works as a Designer where no human eyes can penetrate. Besides the formation of a baby in the womb of a mother, God works in human hearts (minds) to create a new person. Paul puts it this way, "For we are His workmanship, created in Christ Jesus for good works." (Ephesians 2:10) Isaiah describes God as a Potter who forms our lives of clay into something useful. He designs us on the inside to be the work of His hand: perfect and beautiful (Isaiah 64:8) The Designer of man says, "Everyone who is called by My name, Whom I have created for My glory; I have formed him, yes, I have made him." (Isaiah 43:7)

God's ultimate plan as the Master Designer is to have a people perfect and lovely in character, restored to His image and enjoying the new earth. Nothing will mar the beauty of the works of our Creator then. There will be no thorns on the roses, no weeds in the gardens, and no disease. God's original design of symmetry and beauty will be seen everywhere. I want to be among those who walk throughout the new earth and marvel at the creation of God's hands, exclaiming, "How wonderful are your works, my God, how perfect your design!"

Chapter 5

ETERNAL GOD

"The eternal God is your refuge, and underneath are the everlasting arms." (Deuteronomy 33:27)

Moses knew God as perhaps no other man ever has. Moses wrote, "Before the mountains were brought forth, or ever You had formed the earth and the world, even from everlasting to everlasting, You are God." (Psalm 90:2)

All my finite mind can understand is that everything and everyone has a beginning. To comprehend a God who has existed from eternity is impossible. I'm thankful that God is greater than I can imagine; I know that He is big enough and knows enough to take care of everything and everyone. The eternal God is the source of life. I cannot explain such a God, but I can embrace Him and trust Him. I can believe that His arms are sufficiently strong to carry me.

The Bible prophets wrote concerning God, "Have you not known? Have you not heard? The everlasting God, the LORD, the Creator of the ends of the earth, neither faints nor is weary. His understanding is unsearchable." (Isaiah 40:28) "The LORD is the true God; He is the living God and the everlasting King." (Jeremiah 10:10)

Since God is from eternity, He alone can offer what is everlasting: life, love, and liberty. "As Moses lifted up the serpent in the wilderness, even so must the Son of Man be lifted up, that whoever believes in Him should not perish but have eternal life. For God so loved the world that He gave His only begotten Son, that whoever believes in Him should not perish but have everlasting life." (John 3:14-16) "Yes, I have loved you with an everlasting love." (Jeremiah 31:3) "Now having been set free from sin, and having become slaves of God, you have your fruit to holiness, and the end, everlasting life. For the wages of sin is death, but the gift of God is eternal life in Christ Jesus our Lord." (Romans 6:22, 23)

This world holds nothing that lasts, but in Christ, we can each possess eternal life, everlasting love, and forever freedom.

Chapter 6

FAITHFUL, FORGIVING FATHER

"Who is a God like You, pardoning iniquity and passing over the transgression of the remnant of His heritage? He does not retain His anger forever, because He delights in mercy. He will again have compassion on us, and will subdue our iniquities. You will cast all our sins into the depths of the sea." (Micah 7:18, 19)

Danny tossed on his bed, unable to sleep. Discontented thoughts tumbled about in his head. *I'm sick and tired of being Dad's slave. Do this, do that, don't do the other! Every day he orders me around the farm. All I do is work, work, work! I want freedom. Maybe I'll run away. No, I have a better idea. I'll hit Dad up for some money, then split.*

With determination Danny approached his dad the next morning. He was just leaving the house to check on the cattle old James had driven into the pen by the barn last evening. Danny fell into step beside his father. In a demanding voice, Danny said, "I want my inheritance money now rather than when you die."

"Why, son? What's the hurry?" his dad patiently replied.

"Well, I've decided I don't want to be a farmer. I want to move to a city somewhere and find a different occupation. Maybe I'll even become famous. I need money to live on until I find a job I like."

Father said nothing. "Listen Dad, you owe it to me for all the hard work I've done for you the past several years."

Finally, Father answered. "Son, I plan to give you the northern section of land, thinking that rise will be a good place for you to build a house. There is a spring nearby. I will give you some animals to start your flock."

"Didn't you hear me? I don't want to farm! I want to be free of dirt and sweat. I want to travel, see the country beyond your estate. I don't want to live here!" Danny argued.

Father and son stood by the cattle pen. Danny didn't care that his dad was troubled by his words. Rebellious thoughts crowded out any tender feelings he had for his dad. He'd had enough of the farm—cows, sheep, fields of corn, wheat, and barley. Let Andy, his older brother, slave away on the old farm. Again Danny spoke, "You have Andy to help you, besides all the servants. You really don't need me. Just give me what you plan on and I will be gone. I want adventure and some excitement in my life!"

With a saddened heart Father looked at his precious son. His voice breaking with emotion, he said, "Danny, you are free to go. I will not force you to stay. Indeed, I cannot. You have made up your mind. I will sell the acreage I planned on giving you. When the transaction is complete, I will give you the money. I love you son. You are always welcome to come back home."

As the months passed, Father hoped to hear from his son. Perhaps he would tell him about his new job. He wondered where Danny was living and if he was happy. Every morning and evening, Father looked up the road hoping to see Danny. He wanted to be the first to spot him should he ever decide to return home for a visit. *Oh, how I love Danny! I miss him so much! I have so many concerns for my boy.*

A year passed. Father inquired about his son from travelers who stopped by his house for a night's lodging. No one could give him any information. He waited with a longing heart for news about Danny. *If only I could know that my son is okay. Is he even alive?*

There was plenty of work to keep Father busy from dawn until dark. Yet the busy days didn't fill the void in his heart left by the son who had walked out of his life. Each morning and evening, he kept the spark of hope alight in his heart by searching the road that passed by his property. *Maybe today he will come.*

One morning as Father was returning to the house from the southeast field, his eyes automatically scanned the road. He started at the lone figure slowly trudging along. In that instant, he knew it was his son! Forgetting his tiredness, Father took off across the pasture where the sheep lifted their curious heads to stare. Quickly, he rolled under the fence, hurrying up the road. He had waited long enough for this moment. He couldn't reach his son soon enough.

With joyful eagerness Father reached Danny, but what a change! In one swift glance, he took in his son's haggard, ragged condition. The next instant, Father drew his son into his arms. "Oh Dad, I'm sorry. I'm a sinner and not worthy to be your son. But can I come home and live in the servant's quarters and work for you as they do?"

Without answering, Father pulled off his robe and wrapped it around Danny's emaciated body. Next, he pulled his ring off his finger and slipped it onto Danny's hand. Then reaching down to his feet, Father pulled off first one sandal, then the other. "Hold up your feet, son."

Danny protested, "No, Father. Put the sandals back on your feet. I've been walking barefoot for months."

Father insisted until Danny bent down to slip his father's sandals onto his dirty feet, brushing at the tears that filled his eyes. *How could his father treat him as royalty when he was just a bum?*

With his arm around Danny's shoulders, father and son slowly walked toward the house, each lost in his own thoughts. *I will kill the fattened calf and have a feast prepared for Danny. We will have a welcoming party!*

Dad can't be mad at me. He must be accepting me back as his son or else he wouldn't have given me his ring. He loves me, no matter what I've done! As this realization hit Danny, he turned to his father as they reached the front gate. "Forgive me," he sobbed.

"I forgave you long ago. I've been waiting every day for you. Nothing you've done will keep me from loving you. Welcome home, son."

Embracing Danny, his Father clung to him. Danny whispered, "It is so good to be home."

Jesus told this story to convey what God is like. Our heavenly Father is merciful, forgiving, and kind. He gives His children freedom to choose how they will live, but there is nothing anyone can do which makes God not long for them to come home. With longing desire He waits, and like the Father in the story, He acts with compassion and acceptance (based on Luke 15:11-24).

God promises, "If we confess our sins, He is faithful and just to forgive us our sins and to cleanse us from all unrighteousness." (1 John 1:9) When we fail and fall, God does not leave us. His promise of love and forgiveness is for each of us personally. He says, "I will put My law in your mind, and write it on your heart; and I will be your God, and you shall be My child. I will personally teach you, and I will forgive your iniquity and remember your sin no more." (Jeremiah 31:33, 34)

If we had to bear our sins, they would crush us, but Jesus died for our sins, and He forgives our iniquities. Instead of dying under a load of guilt and sin, we can believe in Jesus as our Saviour and Advocate. He offers His blood to pay the wages of our sins. When we ask for forgiveness, we must accept it and forgive ourselves as well as others. "For You, Lord, are good, and ready to forgive." (Psalm 86:5)

Not only is God a forgiving Father, He is also a faithful Father. He is faithful to provide for all my needs, enriching my life by fellowship with His Son. He is faithful to deliver me from temptation and keep in check the trials. God is faithful to take care of me no matter what happens. I can trust what God says, because He is faithful to keep His word. (1 Corinthians 1:9, 10:13; 1 Peter 4:19; Revelation 22:6) God faithfully and consistently meets my emotional, spiritual, and physical needs. He has promised, I "shall supply all your needs according to His riches in glory, by Christ Jesus." (Philippians 4:19)

As I mentioned previously, we operate a greenhouse business growing English Ivy, which we wholesale to florists and garden centers. We never know from week to week what our sales will be, and our expenses, especially for heating in the winter and gas for deliveries, add up to big bucks. However, not once in all the years we've been growing and selling plants have we been late paying a bill or taxes. Several times I've gone to the mailbox and found a check just when I needed it to pay taxes—almost to the penny. Other times a customer will order more ivy, or God will lead us to a new person who decides to buy our product, just when we need the money to cover an expense. When our family needed money for educational expenses, we began growing tuberoses and other field crops to sell. I can testify that God is faithful to provide the needed money so we lack for nothing.

I have seen God at work in the lives of my children, faithfully providing for them.

When our eldest daughter married, we searched for a piece of property where they could live and raise their family. We went on many outings to look at various acreages for sale but didn't find anything worth buying. Besides hunting, we were praying. One evening I asked God, "Please give my children land with woods, garden space, a pond, and fruit trees." I had no idea where we'd find such a place at a price we could afford, but I laid out these desires before our faithful Father.

A few weeks later we were on our way to look at yet another "find" from a newspaper ad, and my husband said, "Let's just swing by and take a look at this piece of property." He turned up a road just a couple miles from where we live and parked by a for sale sign at the top of the hill. As we walked over the nearly twelve acres, I noticed woods, fields, a small pond, and fruit trees. I felt sure that this was it! So did my kids. We stood on the spot where they dreamed of putting their mobile home and committed our wishes to God's working. The owners were willing to come down on their price and all the details were worked out for the purchase.

In May 2007, our youngest daughter graduated from Bass Memorial Academy with high honors. As I celebrated this milestone in Krisanna's life, I remembered back three years to our visit on campus during academy days.

Irdene and I had taken a van load of seventh, eighth, and ninth graders to visit the school. We talked with the staff, absorbed the atmosphere, and prayed about if this was where Krisanna should be. The conviction deepened in my heart that God was leading her to attend BMA. When the winners for scholarships were announced, following a morning of taking tests on various subjects, and Krisanna received several scholarships, I knew this was the school for her. Looking back, I see how faithful God has been in guiding, guarding, and growing my girl through her experiences on the campus of BMA.

I have a difficult time trusting a person who is not honest in their deeds and words. I cannot have a close relationship with someone who doesn't have time to listen to me, nor shows an interest in what is important to me. As the years pass and I've spent time getting to know my heavenly Father, He is Someone I can trust. He wants what is good for me, which may be quite different than what I have in mind, but by experience I've learned that God is a faithful, forgiving Father. I often find myself singing this anthem of praise based on Lamentations 3:22, 23.

Great is Thy faithfulness, O God my Father.
There is no shadow of turning with Thee.
Thou changest not, Thy compassions, they fail not.
As Thou hast been, Thou forever wilt be.
Great is Thy faithfulness! Great is Thy faithfulness!
Morning by morning new mercies I see.
All I have needed Thy hand hath provided.
Great is Thy faithfulness, Lord unto me.

Chapter 7
GRACIOUS AND GOOD

"The LORD is gracious and full of compassion, slow to anger and great in mercy. The LORD is good to all, and His tender mercies are over all His works." (Psalm 145:8, 9)

There's a phrase I toss out to people when bidding them good-bye. "Be good," I admonish. But when I stop to think about it, only God is good. Jesus said this to a ruler who addressed Him as "Good Master."

"Why do you call Me good? No one is good but One, that is, God." (Luke 18:19). So, what do we mean when we talk about goodness? How is God good? *Webster's Dictionary* defines good in these ways: 1) having desirable or positive qualities especially those suitable for a thing specified; 2) having the normally expected amount; 3) morally admirable; 4) deserving of esteem and respect; 5) promoting or enhancing well-being; 6) superior to the average; 7) agreeable or pleasing; 8) of moral excellence; 9) having or showing knowledge and skill and aptitude; and 10) thorough. This adjective can describe a lot of things: good fruit, good book, good idea, good investment, good construction, or a good person. Yet, no one can measure up to the Source of all goodness, and that is God. He is all of these attributes and more. Goodness is a vital part of God's character.

God said of everything He made at the creation of this world, "It is good." (Genesis 1) Only God's power working in our lives can bring forth any good thing. It is He who works in us to will and to do of His good pleasure (Philippians 2:13). "He who does good is of God." (3 John 11) When we do good things for others, it is God's Spirit working through us.

Every good and perfect gift is from above, and comes to us from our heavenly Father. (James 1:17) God promises, "No good thing will He withhold from those who walks uprightly." (Psalm 84:11)I have to believe that if God is good then He wants only what is good for me. I also must realize that the bad stuff that happens in this world is from the enemy, not God. I cling to His promise that "all things work together for good to those who love God, to those who are the called according to His purpose." (Romans 8:28)

God's blessing to Israel also applies to us if we obey His voice. "The LORD your God will make you abound in all the work of your hand, in the fruit of your body, in the increase of your livestock, and in the produce of your land for good. For the LORD will again rejoice over you for good as He rejoiced over your fathers." (Deuteronomy 30:9) At times this blessing may not seem apparent, but the spiritual outpouring of grace and infilling of peace will be realized even when the physical prosperity is absent.

In this world it seems that the bad far outweighs the good. A spouse has an affair, a child rebels, a parent dies, or there's bills piling up and no money to pay. We've all experienced difficult and painful times. Storms cause damage. Relationships crumble. The longed for baby isn't conceived. An accident occurs. A husband leaves and files for divorce.

One Sabbath morning I was leading the Tiny Tot program at our church, but my mind was really with my precious grandbaby lying in the Neonatal Intensive Care Unit connected to machines and a respirator. Besides being born more than three months early, she now had a systemic fungal infection which was killing her. I sang the songs automatically, guiding the children in placing their felts on the board and participating with various activities. In simple words I told them about Jesus and His love.

When we came to the simple song "God is so good," I nearly choked on the first verse, but I chose to embrace the reality of the message as we sang about God answering prayer, God loving us, and finishing with "God is so good, He's so good to me." Whether God healed Michaela or let her die, my lips praised God for His goodness.

Later at the hospital, my daughter and I talked about the hope of the resurrection, and that her tiny baby was safe in God's loving hands. We would trust His goodness and will. God performed a miracle of healing and Michaela lived. I still praise my Father for His gift of life and the opportunity to watch my granddaughter grow, but even if she was resting in the grave today, as is another grandbaby, I have to say God is good. One day I will get to see Michaela's sibling, but for now I treasure her and her brother Anthony.

Friend, in the midst of the bad, which Satan throws at us, we must hold fast to the truth. God is good! During the joyful hours, when there are reasons to be happy, it is time to give God praise for He is good.

God is also gracious. He is courteous and compassionate in His treatment of those who accept His invitation to spend time in His presence. God's gracious manner is illustrated in a story Jesus told.

There was a certain farmer who needed work done in his vineyard, so he set out early one morning to hire men. Finding several who needed a job, the farmer agreed to pay them each a denarius, the usual amount for a day's work. After he had them busy with their job assignments on the farm, he headed back to the marketplace to see if anyone else was willing to work. There was much to be done, more than a few men could accomplish. There he rounded up more helpers and sent them into the vineyard to join the others, promising to pay them a fair wage. Toward evening the farmer ran an errand to the marketplace and noticed a couple fellows standing around. "Why aren't you working?" he asked.

"Because no one hired us," they replied.

"Well, come with me, and I'll put you to work until sunset and pay you what is right."

The crew of men got quite a bit accomplished before sundown, and the farmer was glad. That evening he told his steward, "Call the men together and pay them for their day's work, starting with the last to arrive."

Each man was given a denarius. The last men employed were pleasantly surprised, while those who had labored throughout the heat of the day complained to the owner because they felt he should give them more.

Turning to the one he'd employed first thing that morning, the farmer stated, "Friend, I am doing you no wrong. Did you not agree with me to work for a denarius? Take what is yours and go on home.

I wish to give to this last man the same as to you. Is it against the law for me to do what I want with my own money? Should you be jealous because I am gracious and good?" (based on Matthew 20:1-15)

Salvation is a free gift, and the reward of eternal life is the same no matter how long one has been in the Master's service. Jesus paid the price, and it is by God's grace that everyone who asks will receive a home in heaven and a crown of victory. "But God, who is rich in mercy, because of His great love with which He loved us, even when we were dead in trespasses, made us alive together with Christ (by grace you have been saved), and raised us up together, and made us sit together in the heavenly places in Christ Jesus, that in the ages to come He might show the exceeding riches of His grace in His kindness toward us in Christ Jesus. For by grace you have been saved through faith, and that not of yourselves; it is the gift of God, not of works, lest anyone should boast." (Ephesians 2:4-8) Wow! What a life at the gracious hand of our Father God! No matter how long we labor, Jesus makes us rich!

Sin marred God's perfect creation, but in keeping with His character of goodness, He has surrounded this earth with an atmosphere of divine grace. Through His Son's work of redemption, God's kingdom will be established. The theme of the grace of God will be talked about forever. For eternity God will extend His graciousness to us. With hand outstretched God beckons, "Come, enjoy everything I've created for you."

Now is the time to respond to God's gracious invitation and accept Jesus as the Savior of your life. Allow Him to fill you with His goodness and use the abilities He's given you to minister to the poor, lonely, and hungry.

"When the Son of Man comes in His glory, and all the holy angels with Him, then He will sit on the throne of His glory. All the nations will be gathered before Him, and He will separate them one from another, as a shepherd divides his sheep from the goats ... Then the King will say to those on His right hand, 'Come, you blessed of My Father, inherit the kingdom prepared for you from the foundation of the world.'" (Matthew 25:31-34)

Chapter 8

GOD IS MY HELPER

"The LORD is my helper, I will not fear." (Hebrews 13:6)

"The LORD is my strength and my shield; my heart trusted in Him and I am helped; therefore my heart greatly rejoices, and with my song I will praise Him." (Psalm 28:7)

My alarm sounded, and I rolled over in bed. As the fog drifted from my sleepy mind, I remembered, today was the day I had to take the nursing state board exam to earn my registered nursing license. For two years I'd been attending college, studying to be a nurse. I felt apprehensive, even though I'd spent several weeks studying and reviewing. There was so much to remember.

Reaching for my Bible, I sat on the edge of the bed and prayed, "Please God, I need Your help today. Help me remember what I've learned and to do well on these exams." I opened my Bible at random to read a few verses. Looking down, I read these words in the book of Isaiah. "Fear not, for I am with you; Be not dismayed, for I am your God. I will strengthen you, Yes, I will help you, I will uphold you with My righteous right hand ... For I, the LORD your God, will hold your right hand, saying to you, 'Fear not, I will help you.'" (Isaiah 41:10-13) What a timely promise just for me! Falling on my knees, I poured out my thanks to my Helper, knowing He would be holding my right hand as I marked answers on the exams.

For two days I took the exams for my nursing license, feeling certain that God was helping me. For several weeks I waited for the results. When the envelope came from Nashville, I eagerly tore it open to read the results. I'd not only passed, but had done well. I fell on my knees again and thanked my heavenly Helper.

If I had time to read through all my journals and recall all the times in my life that God has been my Helper, it would be a book in itself. The other day I found a small blue notebook where my husband and I had written about situations where God had helped us. The first entry was from February 2, 1978, written by Irdene during our final semester in college.

"When I started my car on Thursday, one of the valve lifters didn't stop clacking. It had been giving me some trouble but had always stopped. Not this time. My shop teacher told me that valve lifters cost three dollars each—I needed sixteen of them.

"I went to the library and told God all about my need, how I didn't have money to buy new ones. I expressed my faith that He could fix my car if it was His will. I asked God to fix it and thanked Him. I believed that when I started my car it would be fixed. Praise God! It runs beautifully now! This experience is a great boast to my faith in God, my Helper."

On the next page, I had copied this quote: "Our heavenly Father has a thousand ways to provide for us of which we know nothing. Those who accept the one principle of making the service of God supreme will find perplexities vanish and a plain path before their feet…He is able and willing to bestow upon His servants all the help they need." (Ellen G. White, *The Ministry of Healing*, pp. 481, 482) Below it I jotted God's promise recorded in Philippians 4:19, "My God shall supply all your needs according to His riches in glory by Christ Jesus."

Irdene and I looked to God as our Helper in supplying our need for jobs and a place to live after graduation. God provided both, and we began married life trusting Him. For more than thirty years, we've proved Him over and over by laying our needs before Him. It isn't just the biggies, but also the little things that God is interested in.

Other entries that summer included God fixing our fridge, God providing us a small plot of land across from where we lived for a garden, and God clearing away the rain clouds so my laundry would dry. The following year we experienced His leading in finding a mobile home and a place we could rent. My husband worked hard, but he didn't make much money, yet God blessed, and we were able to pay the doctor and hospital bills for the birth of our first child.

While our children were growing up, I opted to be a stay-at-home mother. We lived on one paycheck, which barely met our needs if we budgeted carefully. We grew a large garden, canned produce in season, drove used vehicles, and took simple vacations.

The other day I was recalling how my children thought it was a great diversion to go to what we nicknamed "The Paw Through Store" to shop. A huge pile of clothes was dumped in this room, costing only a few cents apiece. We had fun pawing through the articles, hunting for things we could use. People would give us hand-me-downs, and I sewed dresses. God provided the money to buy our children new shoes each year.

We didn't have much money to spend on Christmas gifts, but God always provided so we'd have a surprise for our children. One year Irdene came home with a doll bed someone had thrown out, which he repaired for our daughter. He made building blocks out of scrap wood and fixed up used tricycles and bicycles we found at flea markets.

When our third child was a baby, we began a plant nursery, raising blueberry bushes and other shrubbery which we sold wholesale. We gave our older children a percent of the money from sales, as they helped me with the potting and watering. It became a family joke that whenever it was a rainy day and we were in the middle of eating lunch, Mr. C. H. would drive in wanting to buy a load of blueberry bushes. Knowing this meant spending money, my kids would don boots and jackets. Together we loaded his old Chevy pickup with pots of bushes. God had provided again!

Through the years of raising our children, I learned that Jesus is a wonderful Helper for mothers. There were days, when at my wits end, I'd lock myself in my bedroom and plead with Jesus for help concerning my children so I could guide them aright. I sought His advice on discipline, but I also asked God for ideas I could implement to occupy my children and help them be happy. There were evenings I'd sit at my desk pleading for wisdom to figure out an algebra problem so I could help my son with his math. Then there were days when I'd stand in the middle of my kitchen with the cupboard doors open and pray for an idea of what to fix for the next meal. I can testify that in every situation God helped me.

Years have passed, and our kids are now adults. We have turned to God to help them find country homes, jobs, money for college, and church families. He's been a faithful Helper. I've also prayed for many people and have seen God step in to help them.

A friend who delivers our gas told us about his experience. Ricky had a stroke that caused him to become nearly blind. The doctor told him he would not recover his sight nor be able to continue working. He turned to his Helper, pleading with God for his eyesight. In sharing his story, Ricky said, "I took a rake and went out into my yard. I raked leaves, and I cried. I prayed, and I cried out to God to give me back my eyes so I could work and support my family. For hours I pleaded with tears to God to restore my sight. God chose to heal me. My doctor was amazed. In a few months after my stroke, I was back on the job. I tell everyone who will listen what God has done for me."

Truly, "God is our refuge and strength, a very present help in trouble. Therefore we will not fear." (Psalm 46:1, 2)

Another friend experienced a different kind of miracle in response to his need. Fred was in a construction accident when a truss snapped and fifteen tons of lumber came crashing down. He was knocked onto the concrete floor, which broke his neck. As Fred lay on the floor, he felt God's perfect peace. When the doctors informed him he would never walk again, he felt no fear. God sustained Fred's spirit and helped him to accept what He had allowed. God continues to bless Fred with a full life even though he is paralyzed. Whether your need seems beyond help, or in many eyes wouldn't be worth mentioning, God cares and wants to help. He's big enough for any job and humble enough to do anything He can to bless us. Don't hesitate to ask.

"I will lift up my eyes to the hills—from whence comes my help? My help comes from the LORD who made heaven and earth. He will not allow your foot to be moved. He who keeps you will not slumber...The LORD is your keeper. The LORD is your shade at your right hand...The LORD shall preserve you from all evil; He shall preserve your soul. The LORD shall preserve your going out and your coming in from this time forth, and even forevermore" (Psalm 121:1-8).

Chapter 9

INTERESTED IN ME

"The LORD looks from heaven; He sees all the sons of men. From the place of His dwelling He looks on all the inhabitants of the earth. He fashions their hearts individually; He considers [understands] all their works." (Psalm 33:13-15)

"For thus says the High and Lofty One who inhabits eternity, whose name is Holy: 'I dwell in the high and holy place, [and] with him who has a contrite and humble spirit, to revive the spirit of the humble and to revive the heart of the contrite ones." (Isaiah 57:15)

These words of God blow me away! The Creator God, who is all powerful and can do anything, not only knows all about me but is interested in me as an individual! He made me unique, a one-of-a-kind creation. And since He made me, He understands how I think. Further, He loves me so much that when I accept Jesus as my Savior He comes to dwell within me. I can't wrap my reasoning around this kind of a God. I just have to accept His Word and give Him praise for Who He is.

God's knowledge of me, as a unique individual, is wonderful and beyond my understanding. "O LORD, You have searched me and known me. You know my sitting down and my rising up; You understand my thought afar off. You comprehend my path and my lying down, and are acquainted with all my ways. For there is not a word on my tongue, but behold, O LORD, You know it altogether. You have hedged me behind and before, and laid Your hand upon me…Where can I go from Your Spirit? Or where can I flee from Your presence?" Of course, the answer is nowhere. The Psalmist continues, "For you formed my inward parts; You covered me in my mother's womb. I will praise You, for I am fearfully and wonderfully made…My frame was not hidden from You, when I was made in secret…Your eyes saw my substance being yet unformed. And in Your book they all were written...How precious also are Your thoughts to me, O God! How great is the sum of them! If I should count them, they would be more in number than the sand. When I awake, I am still with You." (Psalm 139:1-7, 13-18)

At my first women's retreat, I sat in a conference room enjoying the view of a beautiful lake out the front window. All weekend the ladies gathered in this room to sing and worship together, sharing laughter and tears. I'd been blessed by the encouraging messages of the guest speaker, but even though I sat surrounded by more than 100 women, I felt so alone and insignificant.

Just before the final prayer the Women's Ministries leader stood in front of us shaking a basket filled with our name tags. "Whoever's name I draw will win the large wreath," she announced, turning around to point to the vine with white flowers and greenery, which served as the auditorium's central decoration. "The wreath goes to Barbara Kay."

Me? My name had never been picked to win anything! I felt stunned. The opening meeting I'd won a book because it was my birthday. Now I was the lucky winner of the big drawing. It was just too much! I was not worthy of receiving two gifts the same weekend.

As I stood and went forward, God whispered into my ear, "You are special to Me." I knew it was no coincidence that my name was picked. God had a message of love for me individually, and He chose the wreath to say it. Today this lovely flower wreath hangs over my computer table, a reminder of my worth to God.

During my teen years, I longed for a relationship with my daddy and to receive from him words of affirmation. I knew my daddy loved me, but he didn't know how to express his love in a way that was meaningful to me. When I was a young adult, he was snatched out of my life in a tragic airplane crash. During my childhood, my mother was with us more of the time, caring for our physical needs. Yet, she was unable to give me emotional security or "speak" my love language: affirmation. However, she gave me the most important thing; she taught me about Jesus and showed me that I could have a friendship with Him.

As I approached midlife, I began to access my emotional state, discovering the reason for the void I felt. I'd tried filling it in various ways, and came up empty. Finally, I realized that God could meet my inner needs and be the perfect Parent. One day while I was scanning my Bible, reading verses here and there, God whispered a personal message of love and affirmation to me. "I have loved you with an everlasting love; therefore, with loving kindness have I drawn you." (Jeremiah 31:3) These words are my Father's love note to me.

It was at another women's retreat where I felt God's personal touch. A basket of letters was passed around and each lady reached in and took one. Amy had instructed us to find a quiet place to read our love letter from God. I sat on a bank with the lake in view and carefully opened the flowered envelope.

As I read, tears came to my eyes. "I know your heart, My child, even better than you do. I know about each time you've been hurt; for I witnessed each wound as it occurred, and I can see every scar. Through the years, I have healed many of your wounds, but some remain—still tender to the touch. I want to heal those wounds for you too. My healing is not always instantaneous. It can take days, weeks, even years sometimes." Only God would know my inner struggles and quest for emotional healing. The words I read were for my heart alone, a message of understanding from my Father.   S o m e months later, I invited Amy to share with the women at my church. She talked about how God loves us individually and cares for us as His beloved daughters. She had another stack of letters from God. Amy prays over these letters, that each woman will receive the one just for her. I selected a letter and left the room to open it.

As I plopped down on the stairs leading to the youth room I wondered, will God do it again? I glanced at the Bible verse at the bottom, and in that instant, I knew He had. I joyfully read my verse, "I love you with an everlasting love." (Jeremiah 31:3) In the middle of the letter, I read, "I want you to know where My treasure lies. It is you, My child. You are My most valuable treasure. You are what I live (and died) for. Eternal fellowship and relationship with you is worth more to me than anything in the entire universe. I want to spend eternity with you, in a place that radiates with promise and life and joy!" It was signed, "Forever yours."

One day, while browsing in a used book store, I picked up a small book with prayers from God such as Amy had copied to share. From time to time I pick it up and read some of the scriptures and thoughts from my Father's heart.

One evening, I was overwhelmed with several things that had happened to me. I had sprained my foot, and it wasn't healing. I felt discouraged. Seeing *Letters from God* lying on my nightstand, I picked it up and randomly opened the book. My eyes fell on these words, "It Will Get Better." Then in smaller print, "Disappointment diminishes over time." God had spoken to my heart again!

Eagerly I read His message of encouragement. "I have watched you suffer disappointments. And like an earthly father, I long to cradle you in My arms and reassure you that you'll be okay and that before long you will feel better. If you let Me, I can even use your disappointments to strengthen you—to help you grow into the person I created you to be." There were more comforting, compassionate words of assurance and hope.

Many times I've opened my Bible with a prayer that God will speak the words I need, and He is faithful to encourage my heart with whatever passage of scripture I read. I am amazed at how personal God is.

"I have called you by your name; you are Mine...You were precious in My sight...and I have loved you." (Isaiah 43:1, 4)

It is awesome that God loves us so much He was willing to give His only Son to come to this earth and live amid wickedness, battling with Satan and enduring trials. Then Jesus died our death. Each individual is eternally important to our Savior. Yes, I am precious to God, loved beyond measure! So are you!

Chapter 10

IS GOD JUST?

"Ascribe greatness to our God. He is the Rock, His work is perfect; for all His ways are justice, a God of truth and without injustice; righteous and upright is He." (Deuteronomy 32:3, 4)

All heaven was silent. The angels had all been summoned before God's throne. Hushed, they waited, wondering what God had to say. Beckoning His Son to stand beside Him, God spoke, "I am aware of the thoughts that Lucifer has been putting in your minds about Me. He's been saying that I am unfair in not exalting him as I have My Son. There is talk concerning My holy law of love being imperfect. Before I created any of you, my Beloved Son stood beside Me. He has worked with Me in creating each of you, and as the Creator, He alone is to be worshiped and honored. This is My will concerning My Son, and to no one else will I give this glory. My plans are only for Him to know. You are to obey Him as well as Me. I love each of you. I desire your obedience to Me and My Son because you love us. It is your choice."

Subdued, the angels listened with rapt attention. Some were aware of Lucifer's talk against God, but they did not understand the issues involved. God continued explaining the position of His Son and the importance of His law. Finally, God embraced His Son and with a voice of authority declared, "Let all the angels worship Him."

As one, the hosts of angels prostrated themselves before the throne of God. Their hearts thrilled with the spirit of love, and with anthems of praise, these children of God sang with glorious harmony to God the Father and the Son of God.

If only the story ended there. Momentarily Lucifer thought of repenting, but then jealous thoughts again surfaced. Coveting the position of the Son of God, Lucifer continued in rebellion against God and His divine law. Finally, God had to expel His top angel, not only from his position next to Christ, but from heaven itself. With

Lucifer went one-third of the angels.

Harmony was restored in heaven, but the question remained. Is God really just? God has been answering this question for thousands of years, as the experiment with sin and Satan's government continues on this planet. It's a long story. You can read about it in the Bible, where through prophets God records His working of salvation in a world Satan claims as his.

God's justice is always linked to salvation. He says, "A just God and a Savior; There is none besides Me. 'Look to Me, and be saved, all you ends of the earth! For I am God, and there is no other. I have sworn by Myself; the word has gone out of My mouth in righteousness, and shall not return, that to Me every knee shall bow, every tongue shall take an oath.'" (Isaiah 45:21-23)

Christy longed for a baby. She and her husband were able to adopt a son, whom they dearly loved, but she wanted a baby. With modern advances in infertility intervention, Christy and Greg sought medical help. Each month Greg would give his wife injections to stimulate the ovum to mature, hoping that conception would occur. A month came when Christy missed her period and the pregnancy test was positive. She was elated!

Christy planned the nursery. She bought a pair of little booties—pink ones, for the doctor informed her that the baby was a girl. She ate right, took prenatal vitamins, walked faithfully, and daily committed the baby in her womb to God's care.

In the fifth month, when Christy went for a scheduled visit with her physician, her world came crashing down. All was not well with her baby. Tests revealed severe abnormalities. Her baby would not live. Why would God give her a baby in answer to her prayers, only to allow this little girl to die? Where was the fairness of God in all this?

The delivery was a blur of pain and despair. She went through the funeral with a numbness of heart only another mother who has experienced such a loss can understand. Into her pillow at night, she cried tears of bitterness and tears of sorrow. God seemed far away.

Friends reminded Christy of the resurrection morning when an angel would place her baby in her arms. Her baby was not lost to her forever. She would be given back from the grave, whole and healthy. Together Christy and her husband prayed for God's comfort in their deep disappointment and loss. The questions remained, but they decided to continue to trust God.

Maybe you find yourself relating to Christy and Greg with questions of the justice of God. Perhaps you are searching for answers to the tragedies in your life. In this world of sin, none of us is exempt. We are all caught in the crossfire of the great controversy of the ages between Christ and Satan.

Satan attempts to deceive people by telling lies about God. "He's not fair. If God cared about you, He would not have let this happen to you. If God loves you, He would protect you from pain and hurt. Your home would not be burnt to the ground if God was around. Your treasured son would have come home from Iraq. Certainly your husband would not have left you for some other woman. And if God is so mighty and powerful, why isn't He answering your prayers?"

Jesus, who is the Truth, promises, "God is love. God cares for you. He will bear your burdens and hold you close. Even though your loved one dies, one day He will wipe all tears from your eyes and restore your children to your arms. My Father does hear your prayers, and He is at work to bring about His will for your life."

Which voice will we listen to? Reading the first chapters of the book of Job in the Bible will provide some explanation to the fairness of God. You see, God isn't just fair to His loyal children; He is also fair to those who have rebelled against Him, specifically His fallen angel Lucifer, now Satan.

One day God was having a meeting with the "Adams" of all the inhabited worlds He'd created. Satan came as the representative of earth. "And the LORD said to Satan, 'From where do you come?'

"So Satan answered the LORD and said, 'From going to and fro on the earth, and from walking back and forth on it.'

"Then the LORD said to Satan, 'Have you considered My servant Job, that there is none like him on the earth, a blameless and upright man, one who fears God and shuns evil?'

"So Satan answered the LORD and said, 'Does Job fear God for nothing? Have You not made a hedge around him, around his household, and around all that he has on every side? You have blessed the work of his hands, and his possessions have increased in the land. But now, stretch out Your hand and touch all that he has and he will surely curse You to Your face!'

"And the LORD said to Satan, 'Behold, all that he has is in your power; only do not lay a hand on his person.' So, Satan went out from the presence of the LORD." (Job 1:6-12)

Satan had God's permission to hurt Job, and he took full advantage of the opportunity. One day a messenger arrived to inform Job that Sabeans had made a raid and taken away his oxen and donkeys, killing his servants. Right behind this messenger another arrived with word that fire fell from heaven and burned up the sheep and shepherds. As if that wasn't enough tragedy for one day, another servant ran up to Job with the news that three bands of Chaldeans staged an attack, killed the servants who tried to prevent them from stealing the animals, and had ridden off with all his camels. In one day his wealth had been stripped from him.

Then a fourth servant arrived. What else could possibly have happened? The worst thing yet. "Your sons and daughters were having a party at the eldest son's house when suddenly a terrific wind blew fiercely, striking all four corners of the house at once and caused the roof to collapse. All of your children are dead! I alone escaped."

At this final tragedy, "Job arose, tore his robe, and shaved his head; and he fell to the ground and worshiped. And he said: 'Naked I came from my mother's womb, and naked shall I return there. The LORD gave, and the LORD has taken away; blessed be the name of the LORD." (Job 1:20, 21) As Job buried his children and servants, he mourned, but He didn't blame God. He did not lose his trust in the LORD.

God was just to Satan. He allowed Satan to do all these bad things to Job. But Satan wasn't satisfied. Again he came to God's council meeting. The LORD addressed Satan, "'Have you considered My servant Job, that there is none like him on the earth, a blameless and upright man, one who fears God and shuns evil? And still he holds fast to his integrity, although you incited Me against him, to destroy him without cause.'

"So Satan answered the Lord and said, 'Skin for skin! Yes, all that a man has he will give for his life. But stretch out Your hand now and touch his bone and his flesh, and he will surely curse You to Your face!'

"And the LORD said to Satan, 'Behold, he is in your hand, but spare his life.'

"So Satan went out from the presence of the LORD and struck Job with painful boils from the sole of his foot to the crown of his head." (Job 2:1-7)

Job's response to his illness and pain was this: "Shall we indeed accept good from God, and shall we not accept adversity?" (Job 2:10) Job didn't know the behind the scenes plot against him by the adversary. He thought it was God's hand, and in a way, since God allowed it, perhaps it is a fair assumption. Regardless of how one looks at calamity, we can say with Job, "I will trust God no matter what."

I believe God allows Satan to test His children, so that when the war is over, Satan cannot turn to God and accuse Him of being unfair. Even though the tragedies that happen in your life seem totally unjust, remember Job's experience and hang onto the truth—God loves you. The enemy will one day receive his just punishment for all the pain and loss he has caused.

There is a happy ending to Job's story. God restored his losses and gave him twice as much as he had before. He blessed the last half of his life even more than the first, and the exact amount of children were born to him that had died: seven sons and three daughters. It will be the same for each of God's children, if not now, one day in the earth made new.

A song of Moses goes like this: "For I proclaim the name of the LORD.: Ascribe greatness to our God. He is the Rock, His work is perfect; for all His ways are justice, a God of truth and without injustice; righteous and upright is He." (Deuteronomy 32:3, 4) The redeemed gathered before God's throne will sing, "Great and marvelous are Your works, Lord God Almighty! Just and true are Your ways, O King of the saints! Who shall not fear You, O Lord, and glorify Your name? For You alone are holy. For all nations shall come and worship before You, for Your judgments have been manifested." (Revelation 15:3, 4)

Chapter 11

KIND AND CONSIDERATE

"The LORD will command His loving kindness in the daytime, and in the night His song shall be with me—a prayer to the God of my life." (Psalm 42:8)

"I'm hungry, Mama!" little Philip whined. All morning he had sat beside her, playing with some little sticks and grass. For three days Jesus had taught the crowd of people who had followed Him to this quiet wilderness near the lake. They had camped out under the stars, building small fires to cook what few provisions they'd brought with them. Philip's papa and mama had planned to head home yesterday, but Jesus' words fed their spirits and they couldn't leave. Philip liked Jesus' kind voice and happy smile. He told interesting stories, and in the evening, Jesus played with the children.

Mama reached into her pouch, hunting for a piece of bread or fruit she could give her hungry boy. There was none.

"I'm sorry son, but I don't have even a crumb. I'm sorry, but we ate the last of our food at sunup."

Philip didn't think he could wait another minute to eat. He started to cry but noticed that Jesus was looking straight at him. "Before you go home we will have lunch," Jesus stated. This was good news. *Jesus knows I'm hungry*, Philip thought.

Philip watched as a man handed Jesus a basket. From the basket, Jesus took out loaves of bread. Philip counted; there were seven. Raising His hands toward heaven, Jesus asked God to bless the food, and then He began breaking hunks off the loaves. Philip watched with amazement as baskets began to fill up with pieces of bread and the disciples walked among the people passing them out.

"Would you like more than one piece?" a man asked Philip. Shyly, Philip reached out his hands for the two hunks of bread offered him. Quickly, he took a bite, then another, until his tummy was full. It was wonderful bread! (based on Matthew 15:29-38).

Jesus had compassion for the large crowd of people who were far from home with nothing to eat. Jesus wouldn't send them home hungry. He provided food for Philip, thus showing this little boy and a multitude of people that God is kind and considerate of our needs. While on earth, Jesus revealed what God is like by the way He treated people. He thought of their needs, didn't condemn or shame them, and showed kindness to everyone.

I must see this man called Jesus, Zacchaeus thought. He had heard about His miracles of healing and how Jesus' teaching was stirring up many people. Zacchaeus felt convicted about his life of cheating as a tax collector for the Roman government. He took advantage of the people, charging them too much tax and pocketing the extra. Zacchaeus was rich, but he was not happy. He was the head executive in the tax department of Jericho, but he didn't have friends because no one could trust him.

Today, he heard that Jesus was in town and wished to see what sort of person this Rabbi was. So did everyone else. The street was crowded. Being short in stature, Zacchaeus could only see the backs of other men and women. He felt desperate. How was he going to see Jesus? An idea popped into his mind, *I'll skirt the crowd until I'm in front, and then I'll climb one of those shade trees along the road. I'll be able to see Jesus when He passes by. Maybe if I hurry, no one will notice me.*

Settling himself among the branches, Zacchaeus waited for Jesus. He was tired of the life he was living. He longed to be trusted by someone. He wished for peace in his spirit. While Zacchaeus thought about the changes he wanted to make in his business dealings and how he would help the poor, Jesus reached the place where he perched in the tree.

However, Jesus didn't keep walking. He stopped and looked up into Zacchaeus' face. Kindly, Jesus spoke, "Zacchaeus, hurry and come down. I'm going home with you today."

Surprised, Zacchaeus quickly descended from the tree, dropping to the ground in front of the Man he wanted to see. Joyfully he escorted Jesus to his house. Jesus cared about him! Jesus wanted to spend time with him!

Before Zacchaeus could sit down to a meal with Jesus, he stood before Him and confessed his wrongs. He poured out his plans to this Rabbi, knowing He believed him that he did want to change. "Lord, I give half of my goods to the poor, and if I have taken anything from anyone by false accusation, I restore fourfold."

Jesus replied, "Today salvation has come to this house. I came to seek and save that which was lost." (based on Luke 19:1-10)

That day Zacchaeus acknowledged that he was a sinner and accepted Jesus as his Master. Kindness won Jesus a friend for the kingdom. That's how God and Jesus are. They are ever reaching out to the lost—seeking to save. They have the kindest hearts in the whole universe!

It doesn't matter to Jesus what others think about whom He chooses as His friends. To the poor, the lonely, the discouraged, the demon possessed, the lepers, the women and children, Jesus spoke kindly and treated them with respect. No wonder large crowds of people followed Him!

Let me share one more story; this one about a woman. Mary was not a reputable woman. She was known in her hometown as a sinner.

Disgraced, judged, and condemned, Mary was dragged to Jesus' feet in the temple and exposed before those He was teaching. Shame filled her heart. She had been used and abused by men for so long that she looked at herself as unworthy of anything but death. Those religious men had set her up and were now using her in a case to trap Jesus concerning the Law of Moses.

Silently she sobbed, waiting for the verdict of guilty and the pelting of stones that would follow. Through her tears, she saw a finger moving through the dust on the ground where she was huddled. In terror, Mary trembled before Jesus. She was guilty of adultery, but this whole thing was so unfair. The men who had flung her at Jesus' feet were pressing Him for an answer.

Jesus straightened and spoke. "He who is without sin among you, let him throw a stone at her first." Moments passed. No one spoke. No stones were thrown. She saw the finger tracing letters in the dust. Mary felt an urge to grab that hand and hold on, but then it passed. No man had ever protected or helped her. She had to fend for herself, and look where it had gotten her today.

Slowly, Mary raised her eyes, and seeing no one, she stood up. The Teacher was still writing in the dust, and she gazed at Him with wonder. He had the kindest face. He now stood and looked into her eyes. She knew He read her heart and that her fate was sealed. She was a sinner worthy of death.

Smiling, Jesus asked, "Woman, where are your accusers? Has no one condemned you?"

Mary timidly replied, "No one, Lord."

"Neither do I condemn you; go and sin no more," Jesus gently said.

As Mary turned to walk out of the temple court, Jesus turned to those He'd been teaching before the interruption. "I am the light of the world. He who follows Me shall not walk in darkness, but have the light of life." (based on John 8:2-12)

That day Jesus shone the light of His loving kindness to this woman, showing her a way out of the darkness. He gave her hope of changing her lifestyle. He sought to lead her to repentance. Not just her, but also the men who had brought her to Him. Jesus did not proclaim to the crowd the sins of those involved in the plot. By writing their sins in the dust, He could quickly erase them. The accusers found out that Jesus knew their lives. Jesus wanted everyone in the temple that day to repent of their sins and accept His forgiveness. Jesus deals with sinners gently and kindly.

"For God did not send His Son into the world to condemn the world, but that the world through Him might be saved." (John 3:17)

The Bible tells another story about Mary at Jesus' feet. Again she was condemned as a sinner by those who saw her at Simon's feast. Compelled by the Spirit to anoint Jesus' body before He died, Mary had brought the flask of fragrant alabaster oil and slipped into the dining room. She had bought this expensive perfume to embalm Jesus' body after His death, because she believed Jesus' words when He told His disciples that He was going to be killed.

With her heart full of love for Jesus, who had forgiven her sins and cared about her, Mary broke the box and poured out the sweet perfume. Nothing could stop her from sharing this costly gift with the One who had shown only kindness to her.

Words of condemnation reached her ears. That's all Mary had known for so long. Tears flowed down her face, dropping onto Jesus' feet and mixing with the oil. Lost in the moment Mary wiped His feet with her hair, tenderly kissing them. She couldn't stop crying. She heard Jesus telling a story to Simon about two people who owed money. Concluding the story, Jesus told Simon, "Her sins which are many are forgiven, for she loved much."

Jesus spoke softly, "Mary, Your sins are forgiven. Your faith in Me has saved you. Go in peace." (based on Luke 7:36-50)

That evening Mary's doubt about her self-worth was left at Jesus' feet. He not only forgave her, Jesus understood her. She would never forget His kindness to her!

In every kind word and considerate act, Jesus shows us what His Father is like. "But after that the kindness and love of God our Saviour toward man appeared, not by works of righteousness which we have done, but according to His mercy He saved us, by the washing of regeneration and renewing of the Holy Ghost; which He shed on us abundantly through Jesus Christ our Saviour." (Titus 3:4-6 KJV)

Chapter 12

GOD IS LOVE

"God is love. In this the love of God was manifested toward us, that God has sent His only begotten Son into the world, that we might live through Him. In this is love, not that we loved God, but that He loved us. . ." (1 John 4:8-10)

I knew it was time. I knew there was no other way. Tearfully I embraced My Son and held him close for a long time. Then silently I let Him go—down, down, down to the earth where man had rebelled. His place at My side was vacant. The mystery of all ages was happening. My Son became the seed of David in the womb of Mary. For nine months I watched Him grow. The miracle of love lay wrapped in umbilical fluid, quietly maturing. All My love was poured out upon the earth in that tiny, human, unborn boy.

Who would accept Him? Who would appreciate My Gift? Who would receive this baby as the Savior? I watched to see, knowing few would even recognize Him as the Promised One. My Son's life on earth is history now, recorded in heaven for people of all ages to see and read. From an infant in Bethlehem to a Teacher in Galilee, Jesus lived with one purpose, to bless others. My Son loved as none other: unselfishly, unconditionally, perfectly. Yet so many spurned His love, rejected Him, and wanted Him dead.

For thirty-four years, I missed having My Son with Me in heaven. We'd always done things together—designing, creating, and enjoying the works of Our hands. We shared an understanding and companionship uniquely Our own. He had been by My side from eternity, but for a time His place on the throne was empty. You think time drags while you await His return to earth the second time; well, it even seemed long for Me while He was there the first time.

But, I loved you so much that I willingly let My precious, only Son leave heaven to become a man, not just for thirty-four years, but forever. Jesus gave up more than I can explain or you can comprehend, because He also loves you. Forever, He will have your nature. Forever, He will carry the scars of love in His hands, feet, and side. Forever, He will be with you.

One day soon it will be time. Jesus is the way. All of you who embrace His life as your own will have a place at His house. He will come to get you. Down, down, down to the earth, but how different will be His decent. All the beings of heaven will accompany Him. Crowned as the King, My Son will come in majestic splendor. I will send Him with all My love—My beloved Son.

This is God's heart message to you. He could have chosen to wipe out sin every time it arose in the hearts of His created beings. However, if He'd done this, His children would have obeyed Him from fear rather than love. God might have decided not to risk giving His Son. Yet, "For God so loved the world, that he gave his only begotten Son, that whosoever believeth in him should not perish, but have everlasting life." (John 3:16 [KJV])

Love is the very nature and character of God. There is not a speck of selfishness in the heart of our Creator. Love must have expression, so God made angels and beings for companionship. He made us the objects of His marvelous love.

Who can comprehend the love of God? Who can write of His everlasting love? "Behold what manner of love the Father has bestowed on us, that we should be called children of God!" (1 John 3:1) We can see God's love expressed in giving His only Son, but we may also experience God's love personally. Once we do, our testimony will be, "We have known and believed the love that God has for us. God is love, and he who abides in love abides in God, and God in him. Love has been perfected among us in this: that we may have boldness in the day of judgment, because as He is, so are we in this world. There is no fear in love; but perfect love casts out fear, because fear involves torment. But he who fears has not been made perfect in love. We love Him because He first loved us." (1 John 4:16-19)

I've come across individuals who are afraid of God. They believe He lives to take vengeance upon those who disobey Him. They have heard about eternal torment in hell fire, and they decide that if God is like that they won't serve Him. Others claim that God takes their babies away so he can "decorate" heaven with their precious ones. Questions arise, "If God is love, then why does He snatch away my child, plunge my dear one into hell, or punish those who do good to others?"

Before answering these questions in regard to God's character of love, we must take a long look at the cross. Jesus chose to lay down His life to pay the price of sin, which is death, so that He may give eternal life to all who accept His sacrifice. (John 10:15, 28). Father and Son made a provision for sin, because God is love. Jesus didn't die from the loss of blood, the physical pain, or suffocation by crucifixion. Jesus died of a broken heart! God laid on His Son the iniquity of us all. (Isaiah 53:6) Jesus' heart was crushed with the weight of the sins of the world. The blackness of the separation He experienced because of sin is beyond our comprehension. His mental anguish was so profound that He shed drops of blood. Behold God's love at the cross.

In regard to the questions posed above, let me show you from scripture that God is love, "The wages of sin is death, but the gift of God is eternal life in Christ Jesus our Lord." (Romans 6:23) "For He [God] made Him who knew no sin to be sin for us, that we might become the righteousness of God in Him." (2 Corinthians 5:21) Before sin entered this world, Adam and Eve were told that they would die if they touched the fruit of the tree of knowledge of good and evil. The serpent's lie was, "You will not surely die." (Genesis 3:4) Satan has been lying to man ever since, and most of his lies say, "God doesn't love you. God wants to harm you. God doesn't care about you. God is keeping something good from you." All such words are lies. God didn't want his created beings to know evil! He didn't want them to experience death! He wanted them to know only peace and happiness!

God had a plan, a costly, extraordinary plan. Jesus would die in man's place. Thus God would show that He is love. Yes, sin will be punished. Yes, there is a lake of fire that will burn up all who do wickedly until they are ashes. When Jesus returns He will slay all who have sin in their hearts, for sin is consumed in the presence of a holy God. (Isaiah 11:4; Malachi 4:1, 3; 2 Thessalonians 1:5-10, 2:8; Revelation 19:15, 21)

Today, God's Spirit is calling sinners to repent. His heart's message is, "As I live…I have no pleasure in the death of the wicked, but that the wicked turn from his way and live. Turn, turn from your evil ways! For why should you die?" (Ezekiel 33:11)

God doesn't snatch babies away to live with Him. Satan snatches them with disease and accidents, because he wishes to hurt us. Pain and suffering are from the enemy. God grants Satan freedom in this war between good and evil, but it won't always be like this. God promises that one day, "He will swallow up death forever, and the Lord God will wipe away tears from all faces; the rebuke of His people He will take away from all the earth." (Isaiah 25:8)

Jesus refers to the first death as a sleep. Therefore, all who have died are in their graves and know nothing. When Jesus comes with all the angels, He will sound a trumpet and call forth from their tombs those who love Him. Angels will place the resurrected babies into their mothers' arms. Death will be swallowed up in victory! (Ecclesiastes 9:5, 6; John 11:11-14; 1 Corinthians 15:51-55)

The first death can be God's merciful love in allowing the aged to rest. The second death also reveals God's love, because sin will be obliterated. Those who would not enjoy God's way of life and the harmony of heaven He blots from existence. There is no eternal hell fire where the unrepentant burn in torment. God cleanses the earth with fire, wiping it clean of sin, and then recreating it with Eden's beauty. (Revelation 20 and 21) Talking about wickedness and sin, scripture states, "He [God] will make an utter end of it. Affliction will not rise up a second time." (Nahum 1:9)

For the ceaseless ages of eternity, the redeemed will bask in the light of God's love; a love that He bestows on us through Jesus. Like the stream of living water flowing from God's throne, His love pours forth in endless supply, for GOD IS LOVE!

Chapter 13
MERCIFUL SAVIOR

"Gracious is the LORD, and righteous; Yes, our God is merciful."
(Psalm 116:5)

"Through the LORD'S mercies we are not consumed, because His compassions fail not. They are new every morning." (Lamentations 3:22, 23)

Once upon a time there was a king with many servants. One day he decided to look over his accounts, and he discovered that George owed him a huge sum of money. "I've entrusted this servant with business deals, but the figures show he's not been faithful. Bring him to my office immediately," the king commanded.

"You're in trouble," Frank told George when he found him. "The king requests your presence in his office this very hour."

Entering his master's office, George expected to be punished. He knew he'd done wrong by using the king's money for his own project instead of investing it properly, hoping not to be discovered. His venture had failed, and there was no way he could repay. "George, the records show that I'm missing $100,000. What explanation can you give?"

"I lost your money, sir," George mumbled.

The king arose and, looking George in the eye, stated, "You will pay me every cent. If you can't, I'll sell your house and furniture. No, that won't even be enough. I'll have to sell you, your wife, and your children. I doubt that will even be enough for the amount you owe me!" Impassioned, the king waited for George to answer. This was a serious matter.

Bowing before the king, George replied, "I'm sorry, your Honor, but right now, I don't have that much cash. I'm willing to work out some payment plan, as I do owe you the money. Please be patient with me, and I will pay it all back."

Seeing his servant humbled before him, the king felt compassion for George. The king knew he'd never be able to repay that amount of money during his lifetime. "Tell you what. I'm going to release you from the debt. You don't owe me a dollar."

As George left the office, he let out a big sigh. *The king doesn't need the money anyway. He has plenty.*

Within the hour George met up with Harold. "Hey, I loaned you fifty dollars the other day. Why haven't you come by and paid me back?"

Harold replied, "I will bring it to you when I get my next paycheck, but I don't have any money today. I used the money to buy food for my family. Martie was sick, and I've used up all my savings on doctor bills. Please be patient, and I will pay you every cent I borrowed."

"No!" George shouted. "You will pay me this instant down to the very penny!" Grabbing Harold, he dragged him off to the estate prison until he could pay the debt.

Word got around about what George had done to Harold. "It was so wrong of him, especially seeing that his wife is ill. How could anyone be so downright mean?" they wondered. The other servants decided to tell the king what had happened.

When the king heard the story, he was both sad and angry. *I forgave him a huge debt he could never pay, but obviously, George doesn't care. He has no gratitude in his heart or compassion for the plight of others. He will have to be punished.*

So it was that George was put inside the very prison walls where he'd thrust Harold until he could come up with the $100,000 he owed the king.

Jesus told this story to illustrate the principle of forgiveness, but I also see God's mercy displayed by the king's decision. God has pity for our plight, a debt we can never pay. He freely forgives us and accepts payment in full from the hand of His Son. Our King is merciful. Some believe God will not punish sin, but that isn't true. His mercy has a cutoff point, depending upon how we respond. We can accept with gratitude the mercy and forgiveness He offers, or like George, we can slight God and not show mercy and compassion toward our neighbors. Jesus has said, "Blessed are the merciful for they shall obtain mercy." (Matthew 5:7)

Throughout the scriptures are stories of people rebelling against God, disobeying His commands, falling into sin, and making mistakes. In these accounts, I read of how God deals with the erring and rebellious. He sent angels to lead Lot out of Sodom. He didn't abandon the Israelites. He sent messages of entreaty through His prophets, such as this one, "Return to the LORD your God, for He is gracious and merciful, slow to anger, and of great kindness, and He relents from doing harm." (Joel 2:13). Throughout the Bible, we can see a merciful God with hands outstretched to save.

David writes of our merciful God. "The LORD is merciful and gracious, slow to anger, and abounding in mercy. He will not always strive with us, nor will He keep His anger forever. He has not dealt with us according to our sins, nor punished us according to our iniquities. For as the heavens are high above the earth, so great is His mercy toward those who fear Him; as far as the east is from the west, so far has He removed our transgressions from us. As a father pities his children, so the LORD pities those who fear Him. For He knows our frame; He remembers that we are dust." (Psalm 103:8-14)

Jesus understands the weaknesses of humanity, for He became a man and lived where the devil dwells and works. "He had to be made like His brethren, that He might be a merciful and faithful High Priest in things pertaining to God, to make propitiation for the sins of the people. For in that He Himself has suffered, being tempted, He is able to aid those who are tempted." (Hebrews 2:17)

In Christ our Father God has extended a ladder of mercy to this earth. Through His Son He connects us to His eternal throne. We may have fellowship with our God because of His forgiveness and mercy. Jesus tells us, "Be merciful, just as your Father also is merciful." (Luke 6:36) Those who serve the Master and King will live with an attitude of mercy toward their brethren and with a heart overflowing with thanks to our merciful Savior.

Chapter 14

NURTURING PARENT

"As a father has compassion on his children, so the LORD has compassion on those who fear Him." (Psalm 103:13 [NIV])

As a small child, I was terrified of electrical thunderstorms. This particular night, when the booms began, I jumped out of bed and, crying with fear, ran to find my parents. Daddy scooped me up in his strong arms and hugged me against his warm shoulder. "It's okay, sweetheart. You don't have to be scared. Daddy is here."

As the lightening flashed outside the windows, followed by loud cracks of thunder, Daddy held me close. He explained what caused the loud noise, and together we watched the storm out the window. From the security of my daddy's arms, I went from feeling frightened to having a sense of fascination.

That night my daddy gave me a picture of what my heavenly Father is like. Daddy did not scold me for being afraid. He did not insist I go back to bed. He did not tell me to quit crying. Because my daddy loved me and cared for me, he acted with tender kindness. Not until the storm was over did he tuck me back in bed.

There was another picture I received from my parents; this one distorted. My parents seemed too busy for me. As a small child, I remember my mother caring for my three younger brothers, all born before I had my sixth birthday. I know she tried to take time to play with me and let me help her in the kitchen. Still, she put me to bed the same time as my brothers, so I rarely had any special time just with Mommie. Usually, Daddy left for his job before I got up in the morning and often didn't get home until I was in bed at night. I knew my parents loved me, but I wished they had time for me.

I remember a weekend we camped on the beach by the Oregon coast. My Mommie and Grandmother took us children and set up camp Friday morning. When Daddy got off work, he rode his motorcycle to our campsite. We played in the sand, slept in a tent, and enjoyed the beach. When we left for home on Sunday afternoon, Daddy boosted my oldest brother onto the cycle behind him for the ride home. *I'm the eldest, but I am always bypassed because I'm a girl. I wish I could be the one riding with my daddy.*

After some time, Daddy pulled over to the shoulder and stopped. Bud had fallen asleep. He exchanged sons behind him on the motorcycle and off went my middle brother, Bob, for a ride. It wasn't many miles down the road until Daddy stopped again. A sleepy son was lifted back into the car. Baby brother was too young to hang on. "May I ride?" I asked.

Daddy agreed to give me a turn. I didn't fall asleep. I felt excited. We went by his place of work, and he showed me the big machines he used to stitch up camper cushions. Cozy against Daddy's back, my little arms clasping his waist, I rode all the way home with Daddy all to myself.

When I was eight years old, my parents sold our house, and we moved into an old school bus, which Daddy had painted white. Torkey Turtle, as my mother named the white bus, became my house on wheels for six months. It was an exciting adventure to travel all the way from Washington to Chiapas, Mexico. However, at the mission institute, I saw even less of my daddy. Several times, the administration sent him to the United States to bring down a truckload of supplies, and he'd be gone for weeks. They also decided my mother must work in the office, which made her less available to us kids. By the time Sabbath came, my parents were too tired and just wanted to sleep, so often we had to amuse ourselves.

As I grew older, I realized that Daddy's work as a missionary pilot and administrator left little time for his family. Sometimes he would take one or more of my brothers with him to help with some project, but never me. I'd overhear Daddy telling people, "Had us a girl first to be mommy's helper, then I got me three sons." I heard Daddy affirming other people, but I don't remember him saying kind things about me, his daughter. He took time to write letters to other people, but while I was away in school, he never wrote me. I so wanted to be a part of Daddy's life! I needed to hear that I was important to him.

I knew both my parents loved me, and they taught me that Jesus loves me too. I wondered, *does God really care about me, or is He too busy doing all that big and mighty stuff to have time just for me?* With the lifestyle my parents chose, it was difficult for them to have the time to nurture us children. I think Daddy especially was ignorant of how much I needed his affirmation, time, and attention.

From the last two years I was at home, before attending boarding academy in the United States, I have several happy memories of time spent with Daddy. Those years our family was carving out a new mission from the jungle. A river bordered two sides of the property, and many days, Daddy would go swimming with us kids. Several days I worked with Daddy, bringing him mud and bricks for the wall he was building. He even taught me how to lay brick! A few times he let me go with him into town to pick up the mail and buy supplies, giving me a driving lesson in our Ford pickup truck.

Since we were self-supporting missionaries, my father fished commercially in Alaska during the summer to provide money for our family. The summer before I started college, I asked if I could go with Daddy to Alaska, mostly because I wanted some time just with him. I had expectations of having father-daughter talks, going on outings to Walrus Island and other points of interest I'd heard him talk about, and just doing things together. However, I was disappointed to discover that being on the same boat didn't mean Daddy would do things with me. My expectations were dashed. He hung out with other men, and I was pretty much left to myself. He didn't take me anywhere special. He didn't understand my longing, nor did I verbally express it. So I left my teenage years with an emotional hunger to know I was adored by my daddy, accepted by my mother, and affirmed by both as a unique and special daughter.

I was in my early 20s when Daddy was killed. The engine failed, and his airplane crashed in the middle of the jungle. The opportunity to develop a sharing relationship with my daddy as an adult was snatched from me. Because of her own emotional wounds, my mother hasn't been able to be the nurturing parent I need. While she will do anything within her power for me or my brothers, she is incapable of giving me the understanding and emotional support my heart craves. For years, I never realized why I reacted emotionally to situations the way I did, nor why I had such a heart longing that could never be satisfied.

Unconsciously, I sought in other relationships to be nurtured, but what I missed in childhood never came to me from others. Other losses followed as my stepdad died of cancer, and not long afterwards my father-in-law died from Alzheimer's and old age. I looked at the only Father I had left and decided, "You are all the Father I have." As I opened my heart to God, journaling prayers and pouring out my feelings, He began healing my emotional hurts.

My heavenly Father listens to the dreams and desires of my heart and nurtures my spirit. I am able to share with His understanding heart all my sorrows, joys, and desires. God is the perfect parent— nurturing, loving, and caring for me. My little girl heart embraces such a God as my Father. I can run to Him with every hurt, and He comforts me. He encourages me when I am down and counsels me when I ask. He knows what I need as His child to grow in character, so He disciplines me. Through the hard times, He stays with me, and in the happy times, He rejoices with me.

The relationship I share with my Father is intimate and special. He speaks my love language. He affirms me. He always has time for me. God is faithful, loving, understanding, and patient. He gives me gifts—rainbows, flowers, and pets to enjoy. He helps me find lost keys, a music book that is out of print, and a dress for my son's wedding. He even tells me I'm beautiful! Every day my Father blesses my life. I actually believe He is going to spoil me before too many more years pass!

Maybe you are one of the many whose parents have disappointed you. Perhaps you've never felt accepted, affirmed, or understood by your dad or mom. There are fathers who control, abuse, and devalue their children; mothers who neglect, reject, and shame their children. Many parents are unable to show affection or appreciation to their sons and daughters. If we base our view of God upon the experience we've had with our parents, it will be distorted. Even the best parents fail us because they are human, and we as parents fail our children in some way.

Some of you grew up without a father in the home or with a mother who was absent from your life. You didn't get everything you needed from your parents. Accidents and disease have taken parents away from children, and the void is there. Some parents even disown their children, turning them out of their homes to fend for themselves. We can be assured, "when my father and my mother forsake me, then the LORD will take care of me." (Psalm 27:10)

God promises that He will be a Father to us, adopting us as His children and caring for us in a loving, understanding, and protective way. He will also be a mother to His children, for God has the maternal character as well as the paternal. He will never leave us nor forsake us. He is able to nurture us as a perfect Parent. "You, O LORD, are our Father; Our Redeemer from Everlasting is Your name." (Isaiah 63:16)

Chapter 15
OWNER OF EVERYTHING

"For every beast of the forest is Mine, and the cattle on a thousand hills. I know all the birds of the mountains, and the wild beasts of the field are Mine. 'If I were hungry, I would not tell you, for the world is Mine and all its fullness.'" (Psalm 50:10-12)

Jenny yelled, "It's mine!" to which Jimmy responded in increased volume, "No, it is mine!" The yelling match continued, even after Mommy appeared. We are born inherently selfish, and the words "it's mine" play upon our hearts even into old age.

So, is the toy Jenny's or Jimmy's? Is the four-wheeler, motor bike, or car really yours? How about the dresses in your closet, the books on your shelves, or the plants on the windowsill? To answer these questions I want to take you on a world tour with God. Let's start at the beginning.

Stand with me at the dawn of this earth and hear God speaking grass, plants, trees, birds, fish, and animals into existence. Everything God made was good, including man and woman. Eden, the garden of God, was a place of delight and beauty, for it was well watered. In this paradise God created, He made a special garden home for Adam and Eve. The Bible says, "the LORD God planted a garden eastward in Eden, and there He put the man whom He had formed ... Then the LORD God took the man and put him in the Garden of Eden to tend and keep it." (Genesis 2:8, 15)

God told Adam and Eve, "See, I have given you every herb that yields seed which is on the face of all the earth, and every tree whose fruit yields seed; to you it shall be for food." Further God blessed them and told them, "Be fruitful and multiply; fill the earth and subdue it; have dominion over the fish of the sea, over the birds of the air, and over every living thing that moves on the earth." (Genesis 1:28, 29) God gave the first family stewardship of all He'd made. They were to take care of the world for God, which He had created for His pleasure and joy as well as theirs.

Reading on in Genesis we learn how sin entered the world. God had reserved only one tree for Himself. He commanded Adam and Eve not to touch it. They could eat of the fruit of every other tree in the garden, including the Tree of Life, but the penalty was death if they ate from the Tree of Knowledge of Good and Evil. Eve was deceived by a talking serpent that the enemy angel used as his ploy. She chose to obey Satan rather than God. Adam took the forbidden fruit his wife offered and deliberately ate it.

Everything changed. Satan now claimed dominion over this planet and marred its beauty. By interjecting selfishness and covetousness into the hearts of men, Satan has succeeded in nearly obliterating the loveliness God created. Travel around the world and see how man has failed in taking care of the earth. Forests are dwindling. Pollution abounds. Animals are slaughtered. People are shot down. Destruction and devastation is seen everywhere.

Four thousand years after sin entered this world, God sent a Savior. Come with me to a high mountain and watch the drama. The devil has carried Jesus here, and now shows Him all the kingdoms of the world. Hiding the evil, Satan shows Jesus only the glory. Listen as Satan bargains with God's Son, "All these things I will give You if You will fall down and worship me."

Without hesitating Jesus speaks with authority, "Away with you, Satan! For it is written, 'You shall worship the LORD your God, and Him only you shall serve.'" (Matthew 4:9, 10)

Satan had tempted Jesus in the wilderness to turn stones into bread, and then to cast Himself from the temple pinnacle to prove who He was. Jesus, the divine Creator, didn't have to prove anything to the devil. Christ didn't fall under the threefold temptations of Satan, thus enduring the test Adam and Eve failed, which was to trust God's word.

The war that began in heaven between Christ and Satan intensifies as Satan supposes he can overcome Jesus in his human nature. Jesus does not bow. He walks as a servant of God and a friend to man, finally laying down His life on the cross to pay the penalty for sin. God gives the kingdoms of this earth to Christ. Jesus—both by creation and redemption—is the rightful owner.

David writes, "The earth is the LORD's and all its fullness, the world and those who dwell therein." (Psalm 24:1)

Paul reminds us, "You were bought at a price; therefore glorify God in your body and in your spirit, which are God's." (1 Corinthians 6:20)

God and Christ are the owners of the earth and the people who live upon it. We belong to God. We are the property of Jesus Christ. We are stewards of ourselves so taking care of "me" is important. Our children are a heritage from the Lord, a gift to train and guide in His way. (Psalm 127:3) They are God's, and He loves them even more than we do. He gives each child individual abilities and a unique personality. This understanding places responsibility upon us as parents to raise our children as His. We must remember to whom they belong.

Once we grasp that we are not our own, nor are the things we possess truly ours, it will change our lives. Let me illustrate from personal experience.

We have several rows of blueberry bushes, and each summer we enjoy the delicious berries. We eat blueberries off the bushes, I make blueberry cobblers, I pick and bag berries for the freezer, and we pick and sell gallons. Robins also like blueberries, and they come in droves to partake of this delicacy. When these birds return in late summer, they can wipe out the remaining berries in a couple days. I can rant and rave about the thieves, or I can acknowledge that God owns my berry bushes and the robins. The same principle applies when a freeze gets the blooms.

Through the years that we've operated our nursery and greenhouse business, I've come to realize that God is the owner and we work with Him. I can't make a plant grow! We've watched as God has led us to new customers, has had someone call and order just when we needed money, and has worked out the exact income we need each month. The list goes on as to how God has blessed the business.

We drive vans because they have a hauling capacity and can also serve as our family car. They belong to God, although we call them ours because we drive them. God knows each time we need another van, and He has provided. When the one and only new vehicle we ever owned was crunched in a wreck, we were able to purchase another van for just a tad more than our insurance covered. This blue van had a for sale sign in its window for weeks, but God kept it for us. Later my husband came across a maroon van at a nearby car lot for a very low price. We drove it, wondering what could be the matter with it. We had it checked by a mechanic, who advised us that it appeared to be in good condition. We bought it and realized our Lord had just given us a good deal. The same thing happened when the blue van was worn and had a cracked head. God provided another van at a reasonable amount, for which we were able to pay cash. Since these are God's vehicles, we are free to provide transportation to others and leave the money for gas with Him.

Our country acreage, our garden produce, our house are all really God's. I know He has put a fence of protection from the enemy around our property and angels walk on our land. I sense God's presence, and although it is a sin-cursed place compared with the Garden in Eden, it is our haven on earth. God has given us a test, just as He did with Adam and Eve. It is a principle called tithing.

Returning to God a tithe (10 percent) of our increase acknowledges our allegiance to Him as the owner of all. To His people, the Israelites, God commanded, "All the tithe of the land, whether of the seed of the land or of the fruit of the tree, is the LORD's. It is holy to the LORD … And concerning the tithe of the herd or the flock, of whatever passes under the rod, the tenth one shall be holy to the LORD." (Leviticus 27:30, 32) The tithe of the first crops and animals born were to be brought to the Levities, whom God had set apart as the ministers of His sanctuary. The Levites were also to give a tithe as an offering to the LORD. (Numbers 18:26; Deuteronomy 14:27-29; Nehemiah 10:37, 38)

Our culture and jobs differ in this day, but the principle remains the same. One tenth of all we earn belongs solely to God. When we withhold giving God the tithe, it is robbery of Him. When we bring all His tithes into His storehouse, God promises to pour out a blessing. (Malachi 3:8, 10)

When we believe that God is the owner of everything and trust Jesus as our King, praise will pour from our lips as we worship our Creator and Redeemer. "Thou art worthy, O Lord, to receive glory and honor and power: for thou hast created all things, and for thy pleasure they are and were created." (Revelation 4:11 [KJV])

Chapter 16

MY PROVIDER AND PROTECTOR

"The Lord is my Shepherd, I shall not want." (Psalm 23:1)

The tenderest picture of God is as a Shepherd. Jesus says, "I am the good shepherd. The good shepherd gives His life for the sheep." (John 10:11) I have read stories written by those who have raised and cared for sheep, and it has to be one of the most challenging occupations. Sheep are unable to care for themselves in any way. They need a shepherd's constant watch care and provision of a safe place to live and graze. The shepherd's life is wrapped up in the life of his flock through time, attention, and money.

God entrusts men with caring for His beautiful flock, but they often fail to provide and protect. Ezekiel was told to prophesy against the shepherds of Israel: "You eat the fat and clothe yourselves with the wool; you slaughter the fatlings, but you do not feed the flock. The weak you have not strengthened, nor have you healed those who were sick, nor bound up the broken, nor brought back what was driven away, nor sought what was lost; but with force and cruelty you have ruled them. So they were scattered because there was no shepherd; and they became food for all the beasts of the field when they were scattered. My sheep wandered through all the mountains, and on every high hill; yes, My flock was scattered over the whole face of the earth, and no one was seeking or searching for them." (Ezekiel 34:3-6) This neglectful situation is what Jesus referred to when He said, "The hireling sees the wolf coming, and leaves the sheep and flees." (John 10:12)

God says, "Indeed I myself will search for My sheep and seek them out...I will feed them in good pasture...I will make them lie down...I will seek what was lost and bring back what was driven away, bind up the broken and strengthen what was sick." (Ezekiel 34:11-16)

Christ left His Father's house to come among the sheep of Israel and, as the good Shepherd, gather the scattered and battered flock into the fold He called "the kingdom of God." Throughout the gospels we read of Jesus' ministry in shepherding the lame, maimed, and blind. Hundreds flocked to hear His words and to be healed of their diseases. Day after day He provided "food" for the hungry hearts and "drink" for the thirsty souls.

Jesus says, "I am the good shepherd; and I know My sheep, and am known by My own." (John 10:14) The good Shepherd knows each of His sheep individually by name. He knows all about me. He invests in me as His own precious sheep. He is my Provider and Protector. He doesn't leave me to be harmed by a wolf, nor does He neglect my well-being. Under His care I lack nothing.

David, who cared for sheep before he became the king of Israel, wrote of the Lord as his Shepherd. The following is my paraphrase of Psalm 23.

My Shepherd cares for me intimately and completely so that all my needs are met—physically, emotionally, and spiritually. He is enough.

My Shepherd calls me every morning to follow Him, leading me gently to quiet streams where I can drink the life-giving water, then to rest in secluded, fresh meadows and partake of His rich blessings. In this time of solitude, He caresses my spirit and restores peace to my soul.

When I feel refreshed, my Shepherd guides me on a pathway that climbs out of the meadow to a high mountain pasture. Whether He leads me past a cave where a lion may lurk or through a tunnel of darkness where wolves prowl, I need not fear. My Shepherd is beside me with a rod to drive off the predators and a staff to pull me closer to His side. Whenever I'm scared He comforts me by holding me in His arms and speaking words of assurance and hope.

Although the pathway is steep and difficult, it leads to the high places where my Shepherd has prepared me a table of His bounties. Every step of the way I trust Him to take care of me, giving Him my praise and worship.

Finally, we reach the plateau where before me stretches a vast expanse of waving grass bathed in sunlight. Contentedly I begin to graze, knowing my Shepherd is alert to any enemy lurking nearby. Once I have eaten, I lay down, nestling my head in His lap. Gently He massages sweet, healing oil into my scalp. Tired, I sleep. I feel so loved.

Yes, I follow the Shepherd who fills my life daily with His goodness and mercy. I drink from the living water and feast my little tummy on the richest grass, for He has led me to His house. Here I will live forever, baaing out joyful praise to my wonderful, caring Shepherd.

There are many times God has protected me from physical harm. I appreciate His care, and yet I know that He doesn't always snatch us away from danger. Accidents take lives. Daughters of God are raped, abused, and neglected. Men are killed in wars. I read my Shepherd's promise, "My sheep hear My voice and I know them, and they follow Me. And I give them eternal life, and they shall never perish; neither shall anyone snatch them out of My hand. My Father, who has given them to Me, is greater than all; and no one is able to snatch them out of My Father's hand." (John 10:27-29) I have eternal security in Jesus. My spirit is protected by my Father. The enemy may touch my body, but my spirit is safe in God's hands.

I strolled up the road, tears in my eyes and a lonely ache in my heart. I longed for someone to give me words of encouragement. I had no one to talk to but God, and so I cried out to Him. "Look up," He whispered. Lifting my eyes from the pavement, I gasped as I gazed upon the shadow of a cross spread upon the ground. In that moment God reminded me of His love. In giving His Son to die for me, God provided a Man to meet my every need.

It took many years before the message God whispered to my heart that day took root in my soul and I embraced Jesus as my emotional Provider. Now I look to Him to give me understanding, encouragement, fulfillment, romance, and spiritual intimacy. In unique ways, Jesus tells me, "You are special. You are treasured. You are loved."

God is the Provider and Protector of my spirit and heart, and His touch gives me warmth and light. He is your Shepherd too.

Chapter 17

QUIETER OF MY SOUL

"The work of righteousness will be peace, and the effect of righteousness, quietness and assurance forever. My people will dwell in a peaceful habitation, in secure dwellings, and in quiet resting places." (Isaiah 32:17, 18)

Picking up my metal bowl, I left the house to pick blueberries. It was late summer, and I wanted to get enough berries for a couple cobblers before the robins finished striping our bushes. Mechanically I pulled the fruit off the twigs, plunking them into the bowl at my feet. But my thoughts weren't on harvesting or baking, although these were the tasks I was doing. My mind was in turmoil.

I wrestled with the fact that I no longer had control of my child. With enrolling her in a boarding academy, I had entrusted her to the care of others. I struggled with the thought that certain school faculty failed to live what they preached, and some of the "rules" didn't make sense. Our phone conversation kept replaying in my thoughts. Disturbed by what my daughter shared, I felt like jumping in the car to go "rescue" her. Instead, I had calmly listened (which is mostly what she needed) and reminded her to keep her eyes on Jesus, because everyone is human and not always the best example of Christ-like behavior.

My mother heart ached. I longed to protect my child from hurt and being wronged. I ached to hold her, to comfort her. Tears filled my eyes until the clumps of berries blurred. I was upset. I missed my girl. I wanted only good and the best to come to her. I felt betrayed by those adults into whose hands I'd entrusted my precious daughter. I had as many troubled thoughts running through my mind as berries filling my bowl. Finally, I began to pray, telling Jesus about my concerns for my child and how helpless I felt. Then I did what I should have done before hanging up the phone; I surrendered the whole situation to God. There among the berry bushes my understanding Friend quieted my soul. He assured me that He loved my daughter more than I, and He was with her and always would be.

One of my favorite invitations comes from Jesus. "Come to Me, all you who labor and are heavy laden, and I will give you rest." (Matthew 11:28) As I accept and give my concerns and worries to Jesus, He gives me peace and quietness inside. Many times He steps quietly into the chaos of my mind and wraps me in a blanket of peace. Truly, God is the quieter of my soul.

It was a stormy night upon the Sea of Galilee. Jesus and His disciples had set out to cross the lake. Bone weary and exhausted from ministry, Jesus had fallen into a deep sleep, lulled by the rocking motion of the boat. Oblivious to the heaving seas that arose and the blustery wind, Jesus rested securely in His Father's care.

In the middle of the night, the disciples cried out in terror, fearful that they were soon to be plunged into the watery depths to drown. They could not steer the boat, water was pouring over the sides, and their plight seemed hopeless. To this scene of stormy terror Jesus awoke and firmly spoke above the tempest, "O you of little faith, why are you afraid?"

Calmly Jesus rebuked the winds and waves. Immediately the wind died down and the swells smoothed out to ripples. Quietness pervaded the sea and stole into the hearts of the boat's passengers.

This story resonates with my life. Many times I find myself in a "crossing over" experience that doesn't go as I plan. Some storm arises, and I become fearful of the outcome. Time and again Jesus, who is always with me, stands up in the boat and says, "Peace be still."

I've seen my circumstances change under the power of the Word, and my faith has been strengthened. I am learning to trust God as the Quieter of my Soul, turning to Him at the moment the wind begins to howl. When I remember that God is in control, my spirit is at peace even amid tempests.

The blinking light on the answering machine indicated a missed call. Hitting the play button, I listened to the recorded message. It was brief, "Call me. I need to talk to you." Instinctively, I knew that something was wrong.

It was a Sunday afternoon in October, and my husband and I had just come in from the greenhouse where we'd been working. Knowing that our daughter was going on a date with her boyfriend—since it was his birthday—and this call came from his dad who rarely calls us....

We dialed the cell phone number the message indicated. The news was as I feared—bad. Our children had been in a car accident and were on the way to the hospital. That's all they knew, or at least all he was telling us. Silently I prayed that Krisanna would be alright, and I felt Jesus' quieting Spirit filling me with peace. I had no idea how seriously she was hurt or even if she was alive, but I knew she was in God's hands.

I have received many calls, facing moments when I heard the worst news. Like when my mother called to inform me of my daddy's death in an airplane crash. The time my stepbrother called to tell me Dad's cancer had finally killed him. The call one night from my eldest daughter saying she'd miscarried her baby. In every difficult time, I believed God was near. Now as we sped down the road, I committed my beloved daughter to His hand.

We ran into a traffic jam on the interstate, so my husband pulled onto the shoulder and proceeded. It seemed so far to the hospital! Our cell phone rang. The message was hopeful. Krisanna was alive, but they didn't know the extent of her injuries. They thought she was okay. I knew that; God had already told me. Even if she was dead it would be okay, because my Jesus had given me peace about this accident.

In the emergency room I waited for the nurses to bring Krisanna back from an MRI, and finally I was able to be with her and talk to her. The doctor didn't think she had any serious injuries but assured me they'd done X-rays and were checking her out. The next hour blurred as Krisanna began to suffer stabbing pains in her side and a throbbing pain in her neck. I was concerned. This was no ordinary bruising pain, but the ER doctor brushed it off as such. I watched on the monitor as her pulse rate increased and her blood pressure dropped. I wondered about internal bleeding. Instinctively I knew something was wrong.

Still, I felt God's presence in the room and in my heart. I sent up another prayer. Several trauma doctors rushed into the room and quickly informed us that they had just read the scan and it indicated a ruptured spleen. "We are taking her to surgery immediately," the surgeon informed us. A nurse started a second IV, and we accompanied our precious daughter to the doors of the operating room. We sensed the urgency by the quickly called questions of the anesthesiologist as he wheeled her bed through the door and out of sight. I was still at peace.

We found our way down the elevator and through the halls until I stood outside in the evening air. Pulling our cell phone from my pocket, I punched in the phone numbers for our older children. While sharing with them about their sister, who had been rushed into surgery, I attempted to assure them she'd be okay. I wanted my family to have the peace I felt, to know God was with Krisanna. More prayers ascended from various states as the word went around about the accident.

It was a long wait until we finally got the news from her surgeon that she'd come through surgery fine and was in recovery. She would have special care during the night since she was in ICU. There wasn't a bed available in the intermediate care unit so I wouldn't be allowed to stay with her. Tired, but still at peace, I told Krisanna goodnight and that we'd be back in the morning. She was so groggy that I'm not sure our presence sunk in.

As we drove home that night I felt exhausted but very thankful. I knew God was in charge that afternoon, saving the lives of our kids. I still marvel at the quieting touch of Jesus' presence with me. I was never afraid. I give praise to God for all He did that day!

"Be still, and know that I am God." (Psalm 46:10) The Hebrew verb "be still" used in this passage means to cease striving, to become calm. God wants us to take our attention off of ourselves and our distressing problems and focus on Him. I like to slip away to a quiet spot in nature. A bubbling creek sooths my soul, and sunshine beams shining through leafy tree branches calms my mind. In the whisper of wind and singing birds, I sense the presence of God drawing near. In the peaceful places, I am able to listen to my God. "When every other voice is hushed...the silence of the soul makes more distinct the voice of God." (Ellen G. White, *The Desire of Ages*, p. 363)

Elijah was a prophet of God during a time of apostasy. He pleaded with God to turn the nation of Israel away from idols to worship Him. He interceded during the three and one-half years of drought for them to acknowledge God. On Mount Carmel, Elijah prayed for God to make Himself known as the one and only true God. God answered by sending fire to consume the bull, the altar of rocks, and the water with which Elijah had drenched the sacrifice. Following the display of God's power, Elijah entreated God seven times to send rain. He ran before Ahab's chariot while rain poured upon the parched countryside. Then, because he feared the wicked queen's threat, he ran away.

Through the wilderness Elijah journeyed for forty days until he arrived at Horeb, the mountain of God. There in a cave where Elijah slept, the word of the Lord came to His prophet with the question, "What are you doing here?"

At the place where God spoke His law to Israel, amid smoke, fire, and trumpet blast, God again revealed His power. A strong wind tore rocks into pieces, an earthquake shook the mountain, and a fire burned, but God didn't thunder, nor did He rant and rave.

He whispered in a quiet voice. When Elijah heard God's still, small voice, he wrapped his face in his mantle and stood in the entrance of the cave. God reprimanded Elijah for running away, gave him encouragement and instruction for his mission, and informed him that he was not alone in his allegiance to God. (1 Kings 18, 19)

From a crowd to a cave; from Mount Carmel to Mount Horeb; from feeling victorious to feeling despondent, Elijah's experience isn't all that different from ours. To all of His children, whether praying or fleeing, God says, "Be still and know that I am God." He may have to shake the mountain to get our attention, but once we have tuned in to listen, God speaks quietly.

Several years ago I took my Bible, a journal, an inspiring devotional book, and a simple lunch to a nearby mountain. I spent the day walking, talking to God, journaling my heart thoughts, and reading—listening for Him to speak the encouragement my soul needed. Many difficult things were happening, and I needed to un-burden my heart. God met me among the trees and restored my spirit. He didn't give me the answers I wanted, but He let me know that He understood my heart. I returned home renewed from spending time with the Quieter of my Soul.

No matter where we are or the condition of our minds and emotions, God is always available to whisper His words of comfort and admonition. He desires to give us rest, to save us by His strength and power. "Thus says the Lord God, the Holy One of Israel: 'In returning and rest you shall be saved; in quietness and confidence shall be your strength.'" (Isaiah 30:15) Listen to God. Trust Him to be the Quieter of your soul.

Chapter 18
RESTORER

"I will restore health to you and heal you of your wounds, says the LORD." (Jeremiah 30:17)

Since my childhood I've been intrigued by antique cars. Their simple, different look appeals to me. Whenever I see a newly painted antique car going down the road, my wish to own and drive such a vehicle surfaces, and I teasingly tell my husband that I'd like an old Ford for my next birthday.

While some people's hobby is restoring old cars to a state of perfection, and then proudly driving them, others delight in restoring old furniture. Some creative individuals can take old stuff and make something exquisite and beautiful. I have a friend who uses pieces of broken dishes to fashion beautiful artwork designs on platters, lamps, and boxes. Ornate, polished, and artistic items are reminders to me of the masterpieces the Restorer is working to create.

There was a period in my life when I felt drab, like the colors of my life were fading. Changes and challenges left me dull and empty. Questions hung in my mind, the pain of loss surfaced. There were days I didn't want to get out of bed. Emotionally, I felt drained with the demands upon me. I had no human friend to confide in. No one understood the needs of my heart. I struggled alone on the inside while staying busy doing for others on the outside. Crying into my pillow at night, I longed for something different.

The Restorer whispered to me, "I can meet all your needs. My job is to take all the brokenness of your life and make something new and beautiful." I tried to accept His offer, but thought I needed to do some of the work myself. I struggled for a long time before realizing all I was doing was making a mess. Finally, I laid myself in His hands for Him to restore. Slowly I learned to allow God to minister to my spirit, renewing me emotionally and spiritually. This promise became a reality in my life. "The LORD will guide you continually, and satisfy your soul in drought, and strengthen your bones. You shall be like a watered garden, and like a spring of water whose waters do not fail." (Isaiah 58:11)

Restoration is a process, and not all of it is pleasant. Yet, as I rest in the hands of my God, who carefully works with me as His treasure, I have a sense of peace. All the chiseling and molding is to make me exquisitely beautiful. In the process of restoring me to His image, Jesus removes my sins as far as the east is from the west (Psalm 103:12). His work is one of exchanging comfort for despair, beauty for ashes, the oil of joy instead of mourning, and the garment of praise in place of a spirit of heaviness. He makes me righteous, a one-of-a-kind tree planted in His kingdom of grace to bring glory to God. (Isaiah 61:3) Furthermore, He fills me with the fruit of His Spirit—love, joy, peace, and patience. (Galatians 5:22) I praise God for being the mender and healer of my heart.

God is the amazing restorer of relationships. As the Lord restored my spirit, He infused new life into my marriage. Today my husband and I share a richer relationship. We have a new closeness. God is blessing our home with an atmosphere of peace and acceptance. He's at work in other relationships as well, helping me accept people as they are, forgiving those who hurt me, and believing the work God has begun He will complete. God works in ways that to me seem impossible, and for this, I give Him thanks.

The Bible contains stories of people needing the restoring work of God in their life. One such person was David. When convicted regarding his sins of adultery and murder, David prayed, "Create in me a clean heart, O God, and renew a steadfast spirit within me. Do not cast me away from Your presence, and do not take Your Holy Spirit from me. Restore to me the joy of Your salvation, and uphold me by Your generous Spirit." (Psalm 51:10-12) In repentance David cried out to God for cleansing and renewal. From the depths of his heart David entreated God not to leave him. He pleaded with God to be His Restorer.

The truth is, "All have sinned and fall short of the glory of God." (Romans 3:23) Every person needs the restorative work of Christ in their life for we stand hopelessly flawed and broken. Only He can perfectly heal our wounds. God alone is able to make all things beautiful in His time. Our awesome Restorer promises, I will make all things new. If anyone is in Christ, he is a new creation; old things have passed away; behold, all things have become new. (2 Corinthians 5:17; Revelation 21:5)

Chapter 19

STRONG SAVIOR

"In God is my salvation and my glory; the rock of my strength, and my refuge, is in God. Trust in Him at all times, you people; pour out your heart before Him; God is a refuge for us." (Psalm 62:7, 8)

Clutching a tattered and torn shawl around my shoulders, I stand shivering in the dark dampness of a dense forest. I have ventured beyond the boundaries of my parent's estate in search of nuts, roots, and berries. My parents moved away, and the provisions they left behind were soon depleted. For months I've been scrounging within sight of the dilapidated cabin. Now hunger has driven me afar, and with winter approaching, I'm on the verge of despair. Yet, more overpowering than my belly's emptiness is the attack I've just experienced by a smirking being. Sneaking along behind me, darting from tree to tree, he has been throwing insults at me. "You good for nothing, girl. Poor little one. Nobody cares about you. There is nothing worthwhile in your life. You can trust no one. Fraidy lady!" The taunts echo through the wind, constantly piercing my spirit. I feel shattered. I am weak, worn, and worried. I realize I am lost.

As I stumble forward, trying to remember the direction from which I entered these woods, a new enemy appears in front of me, pointing a dagger straight at my heart. Shaking with fright I collapse to the ground and in utter desperation cry out, "Help!"

Instantly I sense a presence. Slowly I raise my head but see no one. To my right a light is shining, and from beside me a voice commands, "Follow the pathway of light. It will lead you out of these dark woods."

Uncertain, I sit up and then stagger to my feet. I wonder how I can continue, weary as I am. Behind me the leering voice of my tormentor squeals, "The lighted pathway will go in a circle. You won't get anywhere. It's a deception. You are too weak to walk anymore."

A soothing voice whispers in my ear, "Trust Me. Follow the

light." I reach down and pick up my ragged, red shawl; then, tossing it around my shoulders, I step to the right and into the pathway of light. Staggering slightly, I put one foot in front of the other, and with each step, I feel a bit stronger. Shortly I lengthen my stride and hope flickers in my heart. Beside me the comforting voice continues encouraging me, "You will make it. You can do it. Have faith in the Light."

After a while I notice a bush with ripe blueberries, so I pause to pluck several handfuls, stuffing the sweet berries into my parched mouth. It seems like the more I eat the more I sense how hungry I really am! Finally I move on, following the pathway of light as it winds between the forest trees and fallen logs. A song emerges in my thoughts, and I hum a simple tune.

> *In the dark I was lost, knew not where to turn.*
> *I stumbled and fell in despair.*
> *But now I am walking, in a pathway of light.*
> *I have hope that someone does care.*

I glance up, and I can hardly believe what I see! Sunshine! Brilliant, inviting, warming sunshine! Through the branches overhead, the sun's rays beckon, and I long to be able to fly straight up into the light of day. I can no longer walk; I have to run. I realize I am nearing the forest's edge. A feeling of joy seeps into my spirit, dispelling the gloom. Although I am alone, I no longer feel alone. As I run toward the light, I rejoice and another song pours from my lips.

> *Praise to the One who made the pathway of light before me.*
> *Praise to the One who sheds the sun's rays upon me.*
> *Praise to the One who makes the light surround me.*
> *Praise to the Lord of Light!*

At the edge of the forest, I stop, surveying the meadow before me. Eagerly I skip into the waving grasses shimmering in the sunshine. Dropping my shawl, I kneel in the fresh greenness, plucking a few blue forget-me-nots from the earth. Turning my face upward, I bask in heaven's light. I sit in the meadow for a long time, feeling at peace. I decide to explore this lovely, lighted meadow where butterflies flit from pink to purple flowers and then on to yellow and orange. The flowers, I discover, are like a rainbow nestled in green, giving me promise of eternal spring. While the tinted, delicate blooms feed my spirit, my belly is still craving food. So, when I come upon a grapevine, I begin popping the marble sized fruit into my mouth, savoring the juiciness. Twisting off one final bunch, I continue wandering in the meadow.

Suddenly the enemy appears, his dagger pointed at my head. I stand there dazed, wondering where he had come from so quickly. How could the evil one be in this lovely place of light? I reach for my shawl, as though it will offer me protection. It is gone! So absorbed was I in the flowers of this place that I'd left it laying somewhere yonder. By now my knees are knocking and my hands trembling. I cannot utter a word. I cannot move. With the dagger before my eyes, I feel horror overcoming me. In that moment the taunting voice from the woods wails, "He's gotcha now! There's no escaping. You are doomed. See what following the light accomplished? Nothing. You are a fool. A stupid fool."

I fall to the ground sobbing and shaking. I know that any moment the enemy will strike. Then I remember, and from my heart, I cry out, "Help!" I continue to lie there, clutching the grass and weeping. Nothing happens. No voice. No noise. No stab. My sobs quiet. Uncurling myself, I slowly raise my head. The light is fading. I am out of the forest but further from the old cabin on my parent's estate than ever, and my enemies lurk nearby. I'm sure once darkness settles over the meadow, they will attack. "I'm not safe even here," I realize.

"What shall I do?" I silently ask, wondering if anyone even knows where I am. To my spirit comes a whispered command, "RUN."

"Where?" I reply.

Just as certain and firm comes the answer, "To the Tower on yonder hill." In the gathering twilight, I strain my eyes to look around me. At first I see nothing but the meadow stretching in every direction, but as I look north it does appear that the meadow slopes upward toward a hill. "RUN," the command comes again.

I dare not delay, for again I hear the shrieking voice, "It's too far! He asks the impossible! You will never make it! Just give up!"

I run, slowly at first, then faster as I feel supernatural strength pouring into my body. As I reach the foot of the hill, the fearful voice calls out, "He'll lock you up in that tower and take all your freedom away. You'll become a slave."

After all I've been through I don't even care what happens to me. Surely what awaits me in the Tower can't be worse than the dark forest, the enemies, and the gnawing hunger I've experienced. "Reconsider where your footsteps are going. The Tower isn't where you really want to spend your life, is it?" The jeering voice seems more frightening than ever.

I listen hard for the encouraging voice I'd heard earlier, but my pounding heart is all I hear. Yet, that whispered command, "RUN," echoes in my mind. I choose to press on. I have to slow a bit as the hill becomes steeper. The Tower looms tall, dusky in the dimming light. I glance back, and now my heart beats with fear. My enemy with the dagger is climbing the hill behind me. "He'll get ya, he'll get ya, he'll get ya," the voice squeaks, sending a chill down my spine.

RUN! I think. "Help me!" I pant in desperation. Then my feet are like that of a deer; it is though I am flying. Before me is an open door, and behind me the screeching voice of my enemy. For a split second, I wonder, "Is the Tower where I really want to be?"

"No!" the enemy shouts.

"Yes!" I reply. I run through the door, which slams shut behind me. I hear the dagger clatter against the metal door, but I no longer hear the jeering.

Instead, I hear the most melodious voice saying, "If you stay inside the Tower, you will be safe. The enemy cannot enter this fortress. I will fill you with the most delicious food, so you never need hunger again." Then, handing me a lovely, white gown the King of the Tower says, "Wear this always." I am mute with happiness, but I manage a smile as I reach out to take the beautiful garment. Then He reaches for me and embracing me in His arms whispers, "Welcome home, my child." I feel such love and acceptance. In this moment I know the Tower is where I want to live forever. I also know that the voice of the King whispering His love for me is the same voice I heard in the woods when I cried for help.

I am shown to a washroom where a central pool entices me to splash in it. Throwing my ragged clothing in a trash can, I jump in, dancing in delighted leaps. I stay here a long time, sitting in the water and dancing by turns. Finally I climb out, feeling clean and refreshed. The gown fits perfectly, as though it were made just for me. As I look at my reflection in the pool, I see a new person.

Emerging from the washroom, I decide to look around the Tower. I notice that it is built of huge rocks, but inside, the walls are decorated with precious stones. The entire premises are bathed in a glorious light. As I stroll around the marble pathways within the Tower, I am impressed with its size. There are magnificent gardens with cascading falls into pure pools of blue water. Beautiful shrubbery and gorgeous flowers adorn every corner. Wonderful, inspiring music plays throughout the fortress.

As I enter a central room I see a long table laden with all kinds of delightful foods. Around the wall are ornate couches, inviting the Tower's occupants to sit and rest. In my eagerness to discover what lies within this Tower of refuge, I've momentarily forgotten how tired I really am. Seeing the soft, inviting couches reminds me. I fill a plate with food from the table; then sink into a plush maroon colored cushion. Finally I can rest. In this Tower on the hill I have entered a place of safety and peace. My belly full, I relax and close my eyes.

When I awaken it is with a sense of perfect peace and a twinge of excitement. I wonder what life in the Tower will be like. For the next several days, I enjoy the beauties within the Tower. I feel at home. The words of the enemy were all lies. Instead of working like a slave, I actually am treated like a princess. In the music of the Tower I hear one message sung over and over—God is love. There are many songs but one pervading theme.

The Tower has become my safe retreat. I never want to leave. Here my needs are met, my heart is satisfied, and I am never hungry. However, I have become a servant, even though I am a princess.

I go out into the meadow, and even enter the forest, to whisper encouragement to other lost souls. I tell them about the Tower on the hill, and if they will run to it they can find refuge from the enemy.

Sometimes the sneering voice pierces the forest with discouraging words. Then I swiftly run to the Tower. And while I run I sing praises to the King of the Tower, and the enemy falls far behind. I've learned that the enemy hates the name of the Tower, so I include that name in my songs. My enemies of fear, insecurities, self-doubt, and worry may holler out in shrieking tones, but they cannot get into the Tower. In the Tower of Jesus Christ I am safe, and I have found rest for my spirit.

"The name of the LORD is a strong tower; the righteous run to it and are safe." (Proverbs 18:10) In this verse the word "safe" has a literal meaning in the Hebrew: set on high. In Christ we are given a place of honor. Paul says it this way: "God, who is rich in mercy, because of His great love with which He loved us. . .and raised us up together and made us sit together in heavenly places in Christ Jesus." (Ephesians 2:4-6) Of those who are in the Tower, God says, "I will set him on high, because he has known My name … I will be with him in trouble; I will deliver him and honor him. With long life I will satisfy him, and show him My salvation." (Psalm 91:14-16) Our eternal salvation is secure in Jesus. He assures us that no one can take us out of His hand. (John 10:28)

Also, in taking the name of Jesus we have His authority and power in our lives. He is our strong Savior. "Whoever calls on the name of the LORD shall be saved." (Joel 2:32) Jesus can save me from negative attitudes such as fear, worry, discouragement, selfishness, pride, jealousy, and discontentment. "The LORD is good, a stronghold in the day of trouble; and He knows those who trust in Him." (Nahum 1:7)

God will give everyone who comes to Him strength to overcome every inherited and cultivated tendency to evil. He is able to deliver you from whatever sinful habit that the enemy uses to bind you. God always answers the cry for help. "Though I walk in the midst of trouble, You will revive me; You will stretch out Your hand against the wrath of my enemies, and Your right hand will save me." (Psalm

138:7) "God is our refuge and strength, a very present help in trouble." (Psalm 46:1)

The allegory is a story of my own life. It is my testimony of a strong Savior. "I will say of the LORD, 'He is my refuge and my fortress; My God, in Him I will trust.'" (Psalm 91:2) I am eternally grateful to Jesus for saving me from the evil one and being my strong Fortress in enemy territory. "The soul that is yielded to Christ becomes His own fortress, which He holds in a revolted world, and He intends that no authority shall be known in it but His own. A soul thus kept in possession by the heavenly agencies is impregnable to the assaults of Satan." (Ellen G. White, *The Desire of Ages*, p. 324)

"If God is for us, who can be against us? He who did not spare His own Son, but delivered Him up for us all, how shall He not with Him also freely give us all things? Who shall bring a charge against God's elect?... Who shall separate us from the love of Christ? Shall tribulation, or distress, or persecution, or famine, or nakedness, or peril, or sword? ... Yet in all these things we are more than conquerors through Him who loved us. For I am persuaded that neither death nor life, nor angels nor principalities, nor powers, nor things present, nor things to come, nor height nor depth, nor any other created thing, shall be able to separate us from the love of God which is in Christ Jesus our Lord." (Romans 8:31-39) From the safety of the Tower, I shout "ALLELUIA!"

Chapter 20
TRUSTWORTHY AND TRUTHFUL

"The Lord redeems the soul of His servants, and none of those who trust in Him shall be condemned." (Psalm 34:22)

"The entirety of Your word is truth, and every one of Your righteous judgments endures forever." (Psalm 119:160)

Yesterday I had the radio on, listening to a news show. They had on some businessman explaining about the oil shortage and economic situation. Earlier in the day, I'd read a lengthy article by a theologian concerning a controversial doctrine. For years I've heard various points about everything under the sun held forth as truth—well, not quite, but enough for me to know that to believe everything one reads or hears is stupidity. So, what am I to believe; who am I to trust?

"You will keep him in perfect peace, whose mind is stayed on You, because he trusts in You. Trust in the LORD forever, for in YAH, the LORD is everlasting strength." (Isaiah 26:3, 4) "Trust in the LORD with all your heart, and lean not on your own understanding." (Proverbs 3:5) "Trust in Him at all times, you people; pour out your heart before Him; God is a refuge for us." (Psalm 62:8)

These inspired thoughts from scripture speak to me of who I can trust: God. I can put my trust in His Word because God cannot lie. (Numbers 23:19; Titus 1:2) Every word from His lips is truth. Jesus is the Word, and everything He speaks is true. Jesus lived by every word that proceeded from the mouth of God." (Matthew 4:4) Of Himself, He declares, "I am the way, the truth, and the life." (John 14:6) Therefore, when I read the Bible, I can believe His message to be the truth.

In this world so many lies are circulating because Satan doesn't want the truth proclaimed. He seeks to trample truth and get people to believe his lies. Of the adversary Jesus states, "He...does not stand in the truth, because there is no truth in him. When he speaks a lie, he speaks from his own resources, for he is a liar and the father of it" (John 8:44). My friend, if you want to know the truth go to the Bible and read Jesus' words. If they contradict what you are hearing, then know that lies have entered your ears. Jesus says, "The truth shall make you free." (John 8:32) Of the Holy Spirit Jesus promises, "He will guide you into all truth." (John 16:13) You can trust God to reveal His truth to your heart.

So, can we trust God? YES! Does this mean that God will do what we want? NO! When I base my trust of God upon the circumstances in my life, I may get caught in the trap of doubting. I read in the Bible Jesus' words, In the world you will have tribulation. The world will hate you and persecute you, just as it did Me. I did not come to bring peace on earth but a sword. (John 15:18-25, 16:33; Matthew 10:34) It doesn't sound like everything will be rosy and sweet, does it? As I've mentioned previously, a cosmic battle rages on this planet, and it is over the question, can God be trusted?

Picture yourself sitting in the Garden of Gethsemane observing Jesus in agonizing prayer. He is pleading, "Oh Father, please take away this cup of suffering for sin from My hand! Is there any other way? I can't do this. I don't want to drink this cup, but Father, Your will be done."

All night Jesus wrestled with the temptation of Satan to give up and leave guilty man to perish. Prostrated on the ground, He struggled and prayed; his anguish was so great that blood dripped from His pores. About His soul Satan cast a dense darkness, tempting Him to think that His Father had forsaken Him. Jesus felt an overwhelming fear of separation from God because of sin. Satan pressed upon Him the lie that if He became the sin bearer for guilty man, He would never again be one with the Father. Never will we understand the immensity of what Christ endured during His baptism of blood.

Years before, Father and Son had covenanted together to save man, and Jesus pledged His life to pay the penalty for sin. Now Jesus chose to cling to His Father, trusting His plan. Jesus would have died in Gethsemane except that an angel came, not to take the cup from His hand, but to strengthen Jesus to drink it. Bearing a message from His Father, "he pointed him to the open heavens, telling him of the souls that would be saved as the result of his sufferings. He assured him that his Father is greater and more powerful than Satan, that his death would result in the utter discomfiture of Satan, and that the kingdom of this world would be given to the saints of the Most High. He told him that he would see of the travail of his soul, and be satisfied, for he would see a multitude of the redeemed, saved, eternally saved." (Ellen G. White, *The Signs of the Times*, June 3, 1897)

Friend, if you are ever tempted to distrust God, spend time meditating on what happened in Gethsemane and at Calvary. Read in the gospels about the day when Jesus laid down His life for you. Consider that a God who loves you enough to give His Son for you to suffer and die can be trusted.

People will let you down. Friends will cause you pain. We are all human and selfish, so of course there are times we will fail one another. At times it feels like God has let us down, but that's a lie. When Jesus hung on the cross, His Father was by His side, veiled in the cloud. We may not feel God's presence, but by faith in His promise, "I will never leave you nor forsake you," we can rest assured that we are never alone.

Satan tempts us to distrust our heavenly Father just as he did Adam and Eve and every human born into this world. However, God is trustworthy, and we can defeat Satan's lies by His Word. "Every word of God is pure; He is a shield to those who put their trust in Him. Do not add to His words, lest He rebuke you and you be found a liar." (Proverbs 30:5)

It is hardest for me to trust God regarding my children. As their mother I've nurtured, protected, and cared for them even before birth. As each has grown and left home on various ventures, I have found myself pleading with God to take care of them, struggling to trust Him when they're out of my reach.

One such time was the summer Irytta canvassed in southern Mississippi with a teen group selling Mega Books. During that time I not only struggled with trusting God to take care of her as she knocked on unknown doors and met all sorts of people, but I asked

Him to give me words of encouragement for my daughter while she was engaged in this difficult work. God's promise for me that summer was, "I will pour water upon him that is thirsty, and floods upon the dry ground: I will pour my spirit upon thy seed, and my blessing upon thine offspring…Fear ye not, neither be afraid: have not I told thee from that time, and have declared it? Ye are even my witnesses. Is there a God beside me? Yea, there is no God; I know not any." (Isaiah 44:3, 8 [KJV]) These assuring words soothed my heart, replacing fear with peace. God would bless Irytta as she witnessed for Him.

As the months of June and July passed, I learned to let go and let God be the constant companion of my child. Irytta prayed books into homes, and her summer experience helped her grow spiritually. Her phone calls home were filled with accounts of "God" moments on the street, and how He used her to plant seeds for the kingdom. He also blessed her with sales, providing money for her school bill.

Several years later I realized that the lessons of trusting God, which both my daughter and I learned that summer, prepared us to trust Him in more difficult circumstances. I shared in chapter one about the miracle of Michaela. Those weeks were one of those times. Trusting God with her precious baby, Irytta continued to pump her breast milk and freeze it. Her faith reminded me of a Bible story I often read to her when she was a little girl. It was one of our favorites.

There was a notable woman who lived in Shunem with her husband, and each time the prophet Elisha traveled that way she invited him in to eat. She even suggested to her husband that they construct a small upstairs room where Elisha could spend the night. Elisha, wishing to do a favor in return for this couple's kindness, asked his servant for a suggestion.

"She has no son, and her husband is old," Gehazi replied.

Calling the woman to his room, the prophet told her, "About this time next year you shall embrace a son."

She was overwhelmed, certain such a wonderful thing couldn't happen. But it did. The Shunammite woman conceived and bore a son just as Elisha had predicted. He was the joy of her life. She felt so blessed as she watched her son grow.

One day the lad went with his father to the field where the men were harvesting grain. After awhile in the sun, his head began to hurt terribly. A servant carried him home to his mother who tenderly held him on her lap until he died at noon. Perhaps it was a heat stroke. Nevertheless, there was nothing the distraught mother could do, so she carried him up to Elisha's room and laid him on the bed.

Wishing to go talk to Elisha, this woman asked her husband for a donkey and a young man to accompany her. "Why are you going to him today?" he asked.

Her answer lets me know she was trusting God. "It will be well."

Hurriedly, she saddled a donkey and bid the youth, "Don't slacken the pace unless I tell you. We have to hurry."

Elisha saw the Shunammite woman approaching and sent his servant out to meet her. Gahazi asked, "Is it well with you, your husband, and your child?"

"It is well," she answered, hurrying on to the house. Jumping down from the donkey, she fell at Elisha's feet. The prophet realized she was grieved about something. The woman poured out her story, insisting Elisha return with her.

When Elisha entered the room, he saw the dead boy on his bed. Several times he prayed to God for a miracle. Finally, the child sneezed seven times and opened his eyes. "Call the woman," Elisha told his servant.

When she entered the room, Elisha smiled and said, "Pick up your son." Joyfully this mother fell at the prophet's feet and thanked him; then she embraced her son (based on 2 Kings 4:8-37).

To say, "All is well," even when one's child is dead shows a heart that is clinging to God's Word and trusting Him.

Everyone has faced trying situations and experienced times when there is nothing you can do except pray and trust God. The trials and tests of life are what give us opportunities to trust God more and depend solely upon Him. In the spring of 2009, I experienced such a time. It was the evening of February 16 when I received the news that my brother, Robert Norton, was missing. During a morning flight, his plane went down in the dense jungles of Venezuela. Over the next few days, our family pieced together what news we could obtain.

Bob, his wife, Neiba, and a teacher from the Adventist school, and recovered patients to drop off in their villages on the way north, had left the Santa Elena airport near the mission to fly to Ciudad Bolivar. That morning a call had come from Karum asking if the AMA (Adventist Medical Aviation) airplane could come and pick up a 14-year-old with appendicitis who needed emergency surgery. Bob's last landing was in that village, where he left a mother and child returning home, and loaded in the sick girl and her mother. He planned to fly on to Bethel to leave the other mother and infant before flying on to the hospital, but let Celso, who does flight following for Bob, know that if the weather wouldn't allow him to land in Bethel, he'd head on for Ciudad Bolivar. The last radio transmission from Bob to Celso was very fast talking, saying the same thing over and over; Celso could not understand the words, so Celso told him to wait five minutes and then try again, which was their normal protocol for bad transmission conditions.

When the morning passed without further communication from Bob, AMA's radio operator reported the downed airplane to the civil aviation authorities, and the search for the missing plane and people began. Eventually, we learned that some Indians had heard the airplane that Monday morning as it passed overhead, but no one knows where it went down. It seems likely there was some problem with the airplane, causing an emergency situation. Since first hearing the news about the AMA plane's disappearance, my family hasn't held out much hope that they would be found alive.

As the days stretched into weeks, I had my own grief to deal with amid the uncertainties, rumors, and waiting for news. As communicator between family members and news sources, I answered phone calls and e-mails that poured in and sent out updates to those on my brother's newsletter list. During this time I struggled with what to tell people. This tragedy was not definable nor explainable, and certainly not understandable.

For nearly eight years, Bob and Neiba have brought life to thousands of the indigenous people in the Gran Sabana area of Venezuela. As a skilled bush pilot, my brother has answered calls for help from many villages, flying out snake bite victims, mothers with pregnancy and birth complications, ill children, and accident cases. The government expelled the other foreign missionaries from the country, but because Bob had dual citizenship and Neiba was born in Venezuela, they could not force them to leave. The real reason Bob was still able to fly was because God was in charge. "This is God's airplane," Bob said in reference to the Cessna 182 he piloted. "I fly for God, and until He shuts us down I will continue doing His work."

From a human standpoint, what happened makes no sense. When the airplane was in the shop for its fifty-hour inspections and maintenance, grounded while waiting on paperwork, or Bob was in the states visiting family, no one answered the emergency calls for help. Before AMA's plane came to their villages many people died. My tears were not so much for myself, but the loss I felt for all those poor people who no longer would have their "Angel of Mercy" to help them.

Satan has tried so hard in various ways to shut down the work of AMA. God has provided many miracles for Bob during his years serving in Venezuela. I don't discount God's power, nor limit His resources. God's hand can stay the enemy, but in the scope of the great battle between good and evil, He does grant Satan power in this earth. In all fairness, the war has to be fought and casualties result. I don't see the big picture, nor do I know what lies in the future. In such times I have to live by faith in Jesus, not by sight, trusting God's Word.

I believe God's Word when He says, "I will never leave you nor forsake you." (Hebrews 13:5) God was with Bob every time He flew. He helped him in landing on very short, rough, one-way, in-and-out bush strips and then taking off again. At times God opened paths in the clouds during bad weather so Bob could land in a village and save a life. I know God was with my brother and the others that fateful morning. Whatever happened, God was present.

The first week as I grieved and wondered what had happened, God spoke to me through this scripture. "He will swallow up death in victory, and the Lord God will wipe away tears from off all faces;

and the rebuke of his people shall he take away from off all the earth: for the LORD hath spoken it." (Isaiah 25:8 [KJV]) One afternoon the next week, I randomly opened my Bible and my eyes fell on this verse in Psalm 116:15: "Precious in the sight of the LORD is the death of His saints." Through these and other scriptures, Jesus has given me words of comfort, affirmation, and hope. I cling to the "blessed hope and glorious appearing of the great God and our Savior Jesus Christ." (Titus 2:13)

The story has not ended. The search continues, both by the Indians who love Bob and Neiba, and by friends doing a technical search on computers from satellite pictures. Regardless of the outcome, I have chosen to trust my heavenly Father. Even though I don't know the answers to all the questions, and even if there is no miraculous deliverance, I still trust God. I continue to pray that God will be glorified and His kingdom advanced.

As we near the second coming of Jesus, things in this world will only worsen. Now is the time to lean on Jesus and learn to trust Him completely. He will see us through the darkest days and lead us safely home to the New Jerusalem where finally the truth "all is well" can be fully and completely realized.

Chapter 21

THE ONE WHO UNDERSTANDS ME

"Great is our Lord, and mighty in power; His understanding is infinite." (Psalm 147:5)

"No One Understands Like Jesus" is the title of a song I often played on the piano, but for many years I didn't grasp the true meaning of these words.

Sprawled across my bed, I reached for my kitty Tigre (Spanish for Tiger). Stroking her soft fur, I poured my heart out to my feline friend. She was my confidant because she had time to listen. Tears dropped onto her striped coat, but she didn't quit purring. Laying my face next to hers, I whispered, "Tigre, you really do understand my heart."

I'd had Tigre ever since she was born to my cat Fluffy, who'd mated with a mountain wildcat. I loved my half wildcat companion! She was a constant in a life of change. Sometimes she'd climb a tree with me, settling onto a nearby branch to survey the scenery while I read a book. Once, my daddy gave in to my pleadings and allowed her and her newborn kittens to travel with us from our home in Chiapas, Mexico, to the United States for the summer. She resided with me at my aunt's house where I spent the summer cleaning in her motel. It was one of the loneliest times of my life, but I had Tigre to pet and share my thoughts with.

When I was teetering between childhood and adulthood, struggling with times of teen turmoil, my precious Tigre disappeared. Her absence stabbed my heart with a deep sense of loss. At that time I didn't have a girlfriend to share with, my parents were too busy and unable to emotionally connect, and now my best friend was snatched out of my life. I had no one who understood me!

One night as I lay in my bed, sleep wouldn't come, only tears. Oh how I missed my kitty! Oh how I longed for someone to understand me! In the stillness of the night, God heard my tears, and He gently caressed my heart. He promised me a special Tigre one day—a big, tame Tigre with stripes and a happy purr. He let me know that He was available to listen.

I guess I've always had a personal longing to be understood and to understand. It is a part of how I'm put together. I've sought it from my mother, my siblings, my husband, my friends, my church family, only to be disappointed countless times. Perhaps I'm too complex a woman, or maybe no one has the time. The reason may simply be that I'm the only one of my kind. It seems that no matter how much I try to explain in order to be understood or seek answers so I can understand, I end up either frustrated or sad.

In my mid-life years, I am coming to realize that only my heavenly Father and Friend Jesus can fully and completely understand me. I'm trying not to expect from others what they are unable or unwilling to give. "I am enough," Jesus reminds me. "I have endured your sorrows, experienced your struggles, encountered your temptations. I know your tears; I also have wept. The grief that lies too deep to be breathed into any human ear, I know. Think not that you are desolate and forsaken. Though your pain touches no responsive chord in any heart on earth, look unto Me, and live." (Ellen G. White, *The Desire of Ages*, p. 483)

Truly my Jesus understands me when I don't even understand myself! Nothing I feel takes Him by surprise for He is intimately acquainted with my spirit. He understands my defects and failings, my needs, and the details of every trial and difficulty. "His understanding is unsearchable." (Isaiah 40:28) God's understanding is limitless; beyond what I can fathom, measure, or know. David told his son, "The LORD searches all hearts and understands all the intent of the thoughts." (1 Chronicles 28:9)

I don't have to fear rejection nor judging from my Jesus when I express my feelings. Whether dejected or carefree, He understands. Twirling amid falling snowflakes, I laugh aloud in my joyfulness. Splashing and dancing in delight, I praise Him in the middle of a summer day from my swimming pool. Running down a trail between lofty trees under the shining sun, I sing. I am free to be myself with my understanding God.

Chapter 22

VICTORIOUS!

"Oh, sing to the LORD a new song! For He has done marvelous things; His right hand and His holy arm have gained Him the victory." (Psalm 98:1)

If you read the remainder of this Psalm, it becomes evident that the writer is referring to Christ's work of salvation for man. As the Son of Man, Jesus learned obedience by the things that He suffered, overcoming every temptation on our behalf. "Having been perfected, He became the author of eternal salvation to all who obey Him." (Hebrews 5:9)

Sin came to the universe when Lucifer, the head angel of heaven whose name means light bearer, coveted the Son's position of equality with God. In his heart Lucifer allowed the seed of envy to grow into rebellion against God. Of him it is written, "O Lucifer, son of the morning! How you are cut down to the ground, you who weakened the nations! For you have said in your heart; 'I will ascend into heaven, I will exalt my throne above the stars of God; I will also sit on the mount of the congregation on the farthest sides of the north; I will ascend above the heights of the clouds; I will be like the Most High." (Isaiah 14:12-14) Lucifer coveted the glory and desired the power that the Father had given to His Son alone.

God called together the entire heavenly population to state His Son's position. "Before the assembled inhabitants of heaven the King declared that none but Christ, the Only Begotten of God, could fully enter into His purposes, and to Him it was committed to execute the mighty counsels of His will. The Son of God had wrought the Father's will in the creation of all the hosts of heaven; and to Him, as well as to God, their homage and allegiance were due." (Ellen G. White, *Patriarchs and Prophets*, p. 36) God bore long with Lucifer, giving him every opportunity to confess that he was wrong and return to his position as the covering cherub, but alas, Lucifer would not repent. The peace of heaven was lost and finally war broke out. (Revelation 12:7) Lucifer and the angels who followed him were cast out of heaven. He became the adversary with a passion to destroy lives and lead all in rebellion against the law of God.

In Genesis we read how God created this world in seven days. He gave to Adam and Eve a garden home and everything in it except for one tree. The Tree of Knowledge of Good and Evil was to be a simple test of their loyalty to God. He commanded them, "Of the tree of the knowledge of good and evil you shall not eat, for in the day that you eat of it you shall surely die." (Genesis 2:17)

First Eve, and then Adam, sinned. Satan, in the guise of a serpent, deceived Eve into believing his lies about God. Both she and Adam failed to trust God and His Word. Before God created beings with the power of choice, He formulated a plan of salvation from sin. It was a costly plan; one that risked all heaven. God would give His Son as a Savior. Jesus is the Lamb slain from the foundation of the world. (Revelation 13:8)

From the revolt in heaven and the fall in Eden, centuries have passed as the war between God and Satan continues. The Bible contains the story of the great controversy. Satan tried in every conceivable way to lead men to worship and obey him rather than God. Satan's accusation against God is that His law is unfair and cannot be kept. God is giving him ample time to demonstrate his style of government. Before the entire universe, God's character is on trial.

In the Bible I read of times when God had to take drastic measures—sending the flood, scattering the people from the tower of Babel, pronouncing judgment upon wicked nations, and sending the Israelites into captivity—so His plan of salvation could be carried out. Then, "when the fullness of time had come, God sent forth His Son, born of a woman, born under the law, to redeem those who were under the law, that we might receive the adoption as sons." (Galatians 4:4, 5)

God's law states that if you sin you die. Paul puts it this way, "For the wages of sin is death." (Romans 6:23) The law condemns, but there is very good news! "What the law could not do in that it was weak through the flesh, God did by sending His own Son in the likeness of sinful flesh, on account of sin: He condemned sin in the flesh, that the righteous requirement of the law might be fulfilled in us who do not walk according to the flesh but according to the Spirit." (Romans 8:3, 4) Praise God! Love made a way! "The gift of God is eternal life through Christ Jesus our Lord." (Romans 6:23)

For thirty-three and a half years, Jesus lived as a human upon this earth. Daily, Jesus overcame the temptations Satan hurled at Him. Satan supposed he would be able to overcome Jesus in His human weakness, but by faith Jesus held fast to His Father's hand and pressed forward in perfect obedience. Jesus showed that God's law can be kept, thus proving Satan wrong. The Son of God developed a perfect character in a world of wickedness. In every way Jesus was victorious!

God sent His beloved Son not only to bear our sins and die our eternal death but to reveal His character of love. "God was in Christ reconciling the world to Himself." (2 Corinthians 5:19) Jesus told His disciples, "He who has seen Me has seen the Father." (John 14:9) By His every word and deed, Jesus showed what God is like. God sets forth His Son as the Light to reveal His character—His law—as holy, just, and good. (Romans 7:12)

Never was God's character of love demonstrated more clearly than upon Calvary. The weight of the world's sin crushed out Jesus' life as He paid the penalty of sin. The watching universe beheld that God's eternal law was unchanging as Himself. If God could abolish His law, surely He would have done so to spare His Son. "In this the love of God was manifested toward us, that God has sent His only begotten Son into the world, that we might live through Him." (1 John 4:9) "God demonstrates His own love toward us, in that while we were still sinners, Christ died for us." (Romans 5:8)

Jesus says, "I lay down My life for the sheep." (John 10:15) It wasn't the torture of crucifixion that killed Jesus. No, He willingly laid down His life as the sacrificial Lamb. He entered the dense darkness of separation from His Father, feeling to the depths of His spirit the agony of eternal loss. It was the weight of your sins and mine that broke the heart of Jesus; "the LORD has laid on Him the iniquity of us all." (Isaiah 53:6)

With His final breath, Jesus exclaimed, "It is finished!" From the cross these words echo to our day a wondrous truth. Jesus died the Victor in the war. No longer could Satan tempt and torture Him to sin. Any sympathies the loyal angels had for Satan and the fallen angels were gone. They saw the price of sin for what it truly was: death. They witnessed redemption's plan as Jesus suffered and died to fulfill God's promise to Adam and Eve.

Over the empty tomb, Jesus proclaims, "I am the resurrection and the life!" Jesus is victorious over the grave! Many will sleep in the dust until His return when the final sting of death is removed, but when Jesus came forth glorified, He was the Victor. His name is to be exalted, and He is to be worshiped as King of kings and Lord of lords. To His Son God gives all authority, judgment, and power to rule. The kingdom is His.

Notice these inspired words regarding Jesus' work. "Now Christ is risen from the dead, and has become the firstfruits of those who have fallen asleep. For since by man came death, by Man also came the resurrection of the dead. For as in Adam all die, even so in Christ all shall be made alive. But each one in his own order: Christ the firstfruits, afterward those who are Christ's at His coming.

"Then comes the end, when He delivers the kingdom to God the Father, when He puts an end to all rule and all authority and power. For He must reign till He has put all enemies under His feet. The last enemy that will be destroyed is death...Now when all things are made subject to Him, then the Son Himself will also be subject to Him who put all things under Him, that God may be all in all." (1 Corinthians 15:20-28)

One day the wicked who have lived in rebellion against God's government and did not accept the atonement of Jesus will be burned up in the lake of fire. Sin will cease to exist, and the earth will be restored as beautiful as Eden. "There shall be no more curse, but the throne of God and of the Lamb shall be in it, and His servants shall serve Him." (Revelation 22:3)

Those who claim Christ's victory will live with Him and the Father in the New Jerusalem. On each head Jesus will place a crown of victory, and we shall reign with Him forever. Jesus shares His victory with us. "The cost of the redemption of the race can never be fully realized by men until the redeemed shall stand with the Redeemer by the throne of God. Then, as the glorious value of the eternal reward opens upon their enraptured senses, and their eyes behold the wondrous glories of immortal life, they will swell the song of victory: 'Worthy is the Lamb that was slain to receive power, and riches, and wisdom, and strength, and honor, and glory, and blessing!.'" (Ellen G. White, *Spirit of Prophecy, Vol. 2*, p. 97) Everyone will throw their crowns at Jesus' feet, attributing to Him all glory and honor as the victorious God. And Christ shall reign forever and ever; Alleluia!

Chapter 23

WARRIOR WHO WINS

"The LORD shall go forth like a mighty man; He shall stir up His zeal like a man of war. He shall cry out, yes, shout aloud; He shall prevail against His enemies." (Isaiah 42:13)

I have an enemy, and so do you. Satan and his evil angels go about seeking to kill and destroy. Their purpose is to enslave and chain a person in bondage. The devil was once Lucifer, the head angel in heaven, but cherishing pride, he allowed sin to corrupt his mind. Now Satan wars against the government of God, running his army with the principles of hate and force. When you were born into this world, you entered a war zone. There are plenty of physical battles going on in this world, but there's also a spiritual war in progress. Paul writes, "We are not fighting against flesh-and-blood enemies, but against evil rulers and authorities of the unseen world, against mighty powers in this dark world, and against the evil spirits in the heavenly places." (Ephesians 6:12 [NLT])

The good news is that I don't have to fight against the enemy! I have a mighty Warrior, Jesus Christ! He fights for me, and He wins! Throughout history Michael, who is the Son of God, has been fighting. He is a Man of war. Of Him the angel host sings in responsive anthems, "Who is this King of glory? The LORD strong and mighty, the LORD mighty in battle." (Psalm 24:8)

"I will not let the people go!" the Pharaoh of Egypt shouted. God had called Moses to lead His people to the land He had promised Abraham, Isaac, and Jacob. The Israelites were in slavery, but it was time for deliverance. The LORD of hosts—God of the angel armies—marched forth to battle. "I will bring you out from under the burdens of the Egyptians, I will rescue you from their bondage, and I will redeem you with an outstretched arm and with great judgments. I will take you as My people, and I will be your God." (Exodus 6:6, 7)

Plagues began falling upon the land: flies, boils, hail, and more. The final judgment was the slaying of the firstborn, and when Pharaoh looked upon the dead form of his son, he relented and let Israel leave Egypt. In one grand Exodus of more than a million people, the mighty Warrior "went before them by day in a pillar of cloud to lead the way, and by night in a pillar of fire to give them light." (Exodus 13:21)

After several days of traveling, the multitude camped beside the Red Sea, and there Pharaoh and his army caught up with them. With 600 chariots driven by captains and thousands of men on horseback, Pharaoh planned to capture his slave labor and force them to return to Egypt. God permitted this advance as a final display of His power to deliver.

Stepping between the enemy and His children, the Angel of God in the pillar of cloud provided light to the Israelites and darkness to the Egyptians. (The Angel of God is none other than the Son of God, Christ.) Moses spoke His message to the trembling people. "Do not be afraid. Stand still, and see the salvation of the LORD, which He will accomplish for you today. For the Egyptians whom you see today, you shall see again no more forever. The LORD will fight for you, and you shall hold your peace." (Exodus 14:13, 14)

God divided the waters, piling them into walls, and created a wide, dry path on which the Israelites walked across the Red Sea. When the enemy army pursued, God fought for them. Wheels came off their chariots, and they had great difficulties. While Pharaoh's army struggled to turn around, because they knew God was fighting against them, God sent the walls of water crashing down. Pharaoh and his entire army perished under the waters.

On the far shore, Moses led the people in a song of victory. "I will sing to the LORD, for He has triumphed gloriously! The horse and its rider He has thrown into the sea! The LORD is my strength and song, and He has become my salvation. He is my God, and I will praise Him; My father's God, and I will exalt Him. The LORD is a man of war; The LORD is His name!" (Exodus 15:1-3)

There have been times in my life when I felt caught between a rock and a hard place. I was totally helpless as the enemy advanced. The spiritual battle is a very real one, but our LORD will fight for us.

He fights for our children. He steps in to fight for our friends and coworkers. God is our Warrior, and when we ask Him to deliver, He is a mighty Man of war.

My favorite warrior story in the Bible is recounted in 2 Chronicles 20. A great multitude from several countries was coming against Jehoshaphat, king of Judah. When the king heard the alarming news, he turned to the LORD for help. Calling all the people of Judah together for a time of fasting and prayer, Jehoshaphat led them to seek the LORD. Before the assembly the king prayed, "O LORD God of our fathers, are You not God in heaven, and do You not rule over all the kingdoms of the nations, and in Your hand is there not power and might, so that no one is able to withstand You?...O our God, will You not judge them? For we have no power against this great multitude that is coming against us; nor do we know what to do, but our eyes are upon You." (verses 6, 12)

The Spirit of the LORD came upon Jahaziel with a message of encouragement and hope. "Do not be afraid nor dismayed because of this great multitude, for the battle is not yours, but God's. Tomorrow go down against them." (verse 15) God gave direction as to where the army was to go and encouraged His people with these words, "You will not need to fight in this battle. Position yourselves, stand still and see the salvation of the LORD, who is with you, O Judah and Jerusalem! Do not fear. . .for the LORD is with you." (verse 17) With thankful hearts the people had a praise service and worshipped God.

The following morning the army assembled and headed for the Wilderness of Tekoa. Jehoshaphat reminded them of the prophet's words and encouraged his army to believe God's message. Then he appointed men to lead in praise singing and their battle chorus rang through the morning air, "Praise the LORD, for His mercy endures forever!" (verse 21)

What happened next is amazing! "When they began to sing and to praise, the LORD set ambushes against the people of Ammon, Moab, and Mount Seir, who had come against Judah, and they were defeated." (verse 22) When the army arrived at the enemy camp, they looked upon dead bodies fallen on the earth. No one had escaped! There were so many valuables that the men spent three days collecting it all. On the fourth day, they had a praise service and blessed the LORD, thanking Him for fighting and winning the battle.

Jehoshaphat led his men home to Jerusalem with rejoicing. Accompanied with various stringed instruments and trumpets, the army marched to the temple singing praises to God. There they worshiped and gave glory and honor to their Warrior for His victory over their enemies.

The testimony of this battle spread far and wide to many countries. "And the fear of God was on all the kingdoms. . .when they heard that the LORD had fought against the enemies of Israel. Then the realm of Jehoshaphat was quiet, for his God gave him rest all around." (verses 29, 30)

God wants us to ask Him to fight our battles and win our wars. He knows our weaknesses and inabilities to conquer the enemy. We can call upon the name of Jesus knowing He is mighty to save. We can trust the power of Christ to give us victory. We can experience peace and rest. Our response to our strong and mighty Warrior God should be praise and worship.

Many years ago Jesus lived on this earth. He fought and won every spiritual battle Satan instigated. When Jesus died He was the winner. In vision John heard a loud voice in heaven saying, "Now salvation, and strength, and the kingdom of our God, and the power of His Christ have come, for the accuser of our brethren, who accused them before our God day and night, has been cast down." (Revelation 12:10)

Although Satan's doom is sure, the battle continues. He lashes out against all who bear the name of Jesus. The spiritual warfare is intense! Listen to this, "And they overcame him [Satan] by the blood of the Lamb and by the word of their testimony, and they did not love their lives to the death. Therefore rejoice, O heavens, and you who dwell in them! Woe to the inhabitants of the earth and the sea! For the devil has come down to you, having great wrath, because he knows that he has a short time." (Revelation 12:11, 12) Through the centuries since Jesus returned to heaven, Satan has persecuted the followers of God, but the mighty Warrior hasn't laid down His sword!

The final war between good and evil is raging all around us, both in the world and in the hearts of men. The enemy fakes strength as he "walks about like a roaring lion, seeking whom he may devour," but he is weak when we claim the name of Jesus. The Lion of the tribe of Judah is the true Lion, and He has a louder roar. (1 Peter 5:8; Revelation 5:5) "The LORD also will roar from Zion, and utter His voice from Jerusalem. The heavens and earth will shake, but the LORD will be a shelter for His people, and the strength of the children of Israel." (Joel 3:16)

In the battles of life, we may trust the Lion Warrior, Jesus, to take care of us, and have faith in the shed blood of the Lamb of God. These Lion and Lamb symbols are powerful reminders of who our Warrior is. Christ is the meek and lowly Lamb, but He is also the powerful and mighty Lion. "Oh, sing to the LORD a new song! For He has done marvelous things; His right hand and His holy arm have gained Him the victory." (Psalm 98:1)

There will be a time in the near future when God will deliver His people from the wrath of Satan. Those who keep God's commandments and hold fast to Jesus will see their powerful, majestic Warrior coming. With an army of angels, He rides forth. "Now I saw heaven opened, and behold, a white horse. And He who sat on him was called Faithful and True, and in righteousness He judges and makes war. His eyes were like a flame of fire, and on His head were many crowns. He had a name written that no one knew except Himself. He was clothed with a robe dipped in blood, and His name is called The Word of God. And the armies in heaven, clothed in fine linen, white and clean, followed Him on white horses. Now out of His mouth goes a sharp sword, that with it He should strike the nations. And He Himself will rule them with a rod of iron. He Himself treads the winepress of the fierceness and wrath of Almighty God. And He has on His robe and on His thigh a name written: KING OF KINGS AND LORD OF LORDS." (Revelation 19:11-16)

In that day Jesus will take the redeemed home as His trophies won in battle. All that will remain throughout the ages of eternity are His battle scared hands, a reminder of what sin cost God and Christ. In the land of perfect peace, where there will never be war again, we will sing anthems of praise to our King forever and ever!

Chapter 24

EXCELLENT IS HIS NAME!

"O LORD, our Lord, how excellent is Your name in all the earth!"
(Psalm 8:1)

One evening during my last year of college, I was sitting at my desk studying. For a few minutes, I let my mind wander to what it would be like when I left my student nurse status to become Mrs. Kay. The previous summer, my sweetheart had asked me to marry him, and I was eagerly anticipating becoming his wife. Picking up a scrap paper I carefully wrote "Barbara Ann Kay, Mrs. Barbara Kay, Mrs. L. I. Kay, and Mrs. Larry Irdene Kay." One day I would sign my name as "Kay," but for now I folded the paper and stuck it in my desk drawer, then focused my mind back on medical procedures.

On May 14, 1978, I stood with my beloved, facing a church full of family and friends who had gathered to celebrate our wedding day with us, and listened as the pastor introduced us as Mr. and Mrs. Larry Irdene Kay. I was married! I could now legally sign my name as "Kay," leaving "Norton" to my birth family.

Names are important because they identify who we belong to. When I hear the name Abraham Lincoln, I immediately think of a great president. Mention the name Hitler and terrible atrocities enter my mind. Say the name Clara Barton and a totally different picture emerges, one of compassion and determination.

In this chapter I want to examine more closely the name of God, which is also His character. The Hebrew word for God is "Elohi-ym," the Supreme God who is Almighty. Written as LORD GOD, the Hebrew word is "Yehovia," which in English is Jehovah, meaning self-existent or eternal. The Jews later also used the name "Adonay," Sovereign Ruler. Comparing the Greek words as translated in the New Testament, the meaning of God's name remains as Supreme Deity and Master (*Strong's Concordance*).

God's name is holy, for He is holy. It must not be used carelessly or repetitiously but with respect and honor. When we take the name of God upon our lips, we are admitting our dependence upon Him and His authority and power. With reverence and praise we'll exclaim, "O LORD, my God, You are very great; You are clothed with honor and majesty!" (Psalm 104:1)

The Son of God, sometimes introduced as the Angel of the LORD in the Old Testament, bears a name that is above all names, yet He didn't usually reveal it. Jacob, the father of the tribes of Israel, was returning to his birth land. He was afraid of his brother Esau that dark night by the brook Jabbok. While praying for protection, a man whom Jacob assumed was an enemy came to him. He shortly realized it was no mere man with whom he wrestled. He clung in faith to "the Man" and pleaded for a blessing. God blessed Jacob by giving him a new name: Israel. Then Jacob prayed, "Tell me Your name."

God replied, "Why is it that you ask about My name?"

Jacob named the place Penuel—Face of God—for "I have seen God face to face, and my life is preserved." (based on Genesis 32:22-32)

The Bible also tells a story of the Angel of the LORD appearing to a woman and promising her a son. In describing His visit to her husband, she said, "A Man of God came to me, and His appearance was like that of the Angel of God, very awesome, but I did not ask Him where He was from, and He did not tell me His name."

To fulfill Manoah's desire to see and hear the Messenger, the Angel of the LORD came again to their home. After speaking with him and his wife, Manoah asked their Visitor to stay for a meal. "I will not eat your food, but you may offer it to the LORD," was His answer.

"What is your name, that when your words come to pass we may honor You?" Manoah asked.

"Why do you ask My name, seeing it is wonderful [remarkable or secret]?" As the goat and grain offering burned, the Angel of the LORD ascended in the flame of the altar! And they fell on their faces and worshiped (based on Judges 13).

To the shepherd Moses, the Angel of the LORD appeared in a

flame of fire in a bush out in the desert. God told Moses that He wanted him to deliver his people from Egypt and take them to Canaan. "When I come to the children of Israel and say to them, 'The God of your fathers has sent me to you,' and they ask me, 'What is His name,' what should I say to them?

"And God said to Moses, 'I AM WHO I AM.' And He said, 'Thus you shall say to the children of Israel, 'I AM has sent me to you.'" (Exodus 3:13-14) Throughout their travels in the wilderness, the Angel of the LORD led the Israelites. God's presence was in the cloudy pillar that went before the people, providing shade during the day and light at night. (Exodus 13:21, 22; 32:34; 33:14)

While on earth as the Son of Man, Jesus stated, "Before Abraham was, I AM." (John 8:58) This was His answer to the Jew's questioning of who He was. Even though He took the form of an angel and then became a human, Jesus is still the divine Son of God. The One who exists as God is the "I AM," not only to Abraham, Moses, and ancient Israel, but to us as well.

Following Israel's sin at Sinai, when they made and worshiped a golden calf, Moses asked God, "Please, show me Your glory." He needed the assurance of God's acceptance and continued presence as their Leader.

In reply God told Moses, "I will proclaim the name of the LORD before you...but you cannot see My face, for no man shall see Me, and live." (Exodus 33:19, 20)

The next day on the mountain God put Moses in a cleft of a rock and covered him with His hand until He'd passed by, allowing His servant to see His back. "And the LORD passed before him and proclaimed, 'The LORD, the LORD God, merciful and gracious, longsuffering, and abounding in goodness and truth, keeping mercy for thousands, forgiving iniquity and transgression and sin, by no means clearing the guilty." (Exodus 34:6, 7)

Moses' response to God's revelation was to bow his head toward the earth and worship. When we grasp the remarkable, wonderful name of our LORD and God our response will be the same. We cannot see God and live, but when we meditate on His name, His character, we will see His beauty, strength, and greatness.

Of Jesus it is said, "His name will be called Wonderful, Counselor, Mighty God, Everlasting Father, Prince of Peace." (Isaiah 9:6) His name shall be called Immanuel, which being interpreted is, "God with us." (Isaiah 7:14, 8:8,10; Matthew 1:23)

Joseph was instructed by an angel in a dream that the child begotten in the womb of Mary was of the Holy Spirit and that "she will bring forth a Son, and you shall call His name JESUS, for He will save His people from their sins." (Matthew 1:21) Jesus was a commonly used name in those days, but the meaning of the name Jesus is profound. Jesus means Savior. "Nor is there salvation in any other, for there is no other name under heaven given among men by which we must be saved." (Acts 4:12) "Therefore God also has highly exalted Him and given Him the name which is above every name, that at the name of Jesus every knee should bow...and that every tongue should confess that Jesus Christ is Lord, to the glory of God the Father." (Philippians 2:9-11)

It's an awesome truth that when I accepted Jesus as my Savior God adopted me as His child and gave me His name! I am His beloved daughter! Married to Jesus Christ my Lord, I carry His name—Christian. When Jesus comes for His own and transports them to His home in heaven, each of the redeemed will have God the Father's name written on their foreheads. (Revelation 14:1, 22:4)

Jesus is a wonderful name! Truly God's name is glorious and excellent! "Oh, magnify the LORD with me, and let us exalt His name together." (Psalm 34:3)

Chapter 25

YEARNING FOR YOU

"The Lord is not slow in keeping His promise, as some understand slowness. He is patient with you, not wanting anyone to perish but everyone to come to repentance." (2 Peter 3:9 [NIV])

The night is dark without even a sliver of moon. Wolves prowl among the rocky ravines, sniffing for an unwary rabbit. A lonely owl hoots his mournful cry. In the distance thunder rumbles. Holding a torch firmly in his left hand, the Shepherd carefully feels his way with the staff in his right hand, carefully navigating between boulders and brambles as he climbs.

He pauses to listen. Hearing nothing besides his own deep breathing and pounding heart, he continues. While his Shamiah is lost, the Shepherd will not rest. He will relentlessly pursue the desire of his heart, the sheep he loves, until she is found. It doesn't even enter his mind about the foolishness of her straying from his side, nor does he plan to reprimand her once she is safe from harm. Yearning for Shamiah draws him onward.

All night the Shepherd searches. He will not give up. As the dark of night slinks away and the rays of dawn creep over the mountain, the Shepherd hears a faint "baaaaa." Quickly he throws down the torch and staff. Scrambling down the embankment toward the desperate cry of little Shamiah, the Shepherd rejoices that she is still alive. He finds her wedged between two rocks.

Gently prying her loose, the Shepherd lifts Shamiah into his arms and sits down upon the rock. Pulling a flask of ointment from his jacket pocket, he pours it onto the tired sheep's head and gently massages it in. He also rubs some into the scrapes on her legs, all the time speaking soothing words to Shamiah. Using his jacket, the Shepherd ties the sheep onto his back, enabling him to use both hands to climb out of the ravine.

At the top he gathers Shamiah in his arms and carries her homeward. She nestles her head against his strong arm, closes her eyes, and rests. The yearning of two hearts has met upon the mountain.

Whether you are a sheep who is lost in the night or one who has been rescued from the chasm on the mountainside, God's heart longs to have you safe with Him for always. God so loved YOU that He gave His only-begotten Son, so that if YOU believe in Him YOU will not perish but have everlasting life (John 3:16). God sent His Son on a rescue mission to save sinners. Jesus, the Good Shepherd, says, "I've come to seek and to save what was lost." (Luke 19:10)

"The heart of God yearns over His earthly children with a love stronger than death. In giving up His Son, He has poured out to us all heaven in one gift. The Saviour's life and death and intercession, the ministry of angels, the pleading of the Spirit, the Father working above and through all, the unceasing interest of heavenly beings,—all are enlisted in behalf of man's redemption." (Ellen G. White, *Steps to Christ*, p. 21)

The heart of the Son of God beats in unison with the Father's heart. Jesus said, "Anyone who has seen me has seen the Father." (John 14:9) God has been misrepresented as harsh and severe, a God who is angry with sinners. Jesus came to remove this misconception of God and reveal the true character of His Father. God's yearning heart for man's salvation was daily demonstrated in the ministry of Jesus.

It was a sultry morning in Samaria. Before dawn Jesus had slipped away from the house where his disciples still slept to commune with His Father. He needed strength and direction for the day. "To whom shall I minister? Show Me, O Father, the one who wants to know You."

The answer to His prayer that morning involved a long walk through the dusty countryside. It was nearing noon as Jesus and His disciples reached a well on the outskirts of a Samaritan village. "I'll rest here while you go buy food for lunch." Jesus waved His disciples on.

Leaning against the rock casing, Jesus prayed. "Father, You brought Me to this spot; now bring me the person who Your heart is yearning to save." Raising His head Jesus' eyes rested upon a woman approaching the well. It was unusual for a woman to come alone in the middle of the day to draw water. Yes, this must be the one who is truly thirsting for the Savior.

"Please, may I have a drink of water?" Jesus politely requested. Surprised, Andriah exclaimed, "Why are you, a Jewish man, asking me, a Samaritan woman, for a drink!" This just was not done.

"If you knew the gift God wants to give you, and who I am, you would ask Me for a drink of living water," Jesus gently replied.

"Are you greater than our prophet Jacob who dug us this well?" Andriah questioned.

"When you drink this water you'll be thirsty again, but the water I offer to you is living water that will quench your thirst forever, and be as a well of water overflowing in your heart with abundant, eternal life," Jesus promised.

"Give me this water!" Andriah felt a new stirring in her heart.

"Go get your husband and come back," Jesus instructed.

"But I don't have a husband," she replied.

"You are right, yet you've had five, and the man you are with now is not your husband." Jesus sought to bring conviction to the woman's heart, both of her need and of who He was.

Wondering how this Man knew about her life, Andriah stated, "You must be a prophet."

After a bit more conversation, Andriah hurried into town to tell about the Man she'd met at the well. "He told me everything I've done! Could this be the Christ?"

That evening and for the next two days, Jesus taught Andriah and her townspeople about the kingdom of God. As He imparted to their thirsty souls living water, His yearning heart was satisfied (based on John 4:1-42).

Some time later Jesus was in Jerusalem. He'd just been run out of the temple by a mob of distraught Jews who didn't want to believe that He was the Son of God. They'd picked up stones to kill Him, but He'd slipped out under the protective escort of angels. Now, as He was walking up the street, He noticed a man who'd been blind from birth. Jesus' heart yearned to restore not just his physical sight, but also to give him spiritual eyesight. Turning to His disciples, Jesus shared, "I must work for my Father today, for I am the light of the world."

What Jesus did next continues to puzzle me. He spat on the ground and made clay with the saliva. Reaching out to the blind man, Jesus daubed slimy mud upon his eyes, and then sent him to wash it off in the pool of Siloam. There was no magical power in the saliva from Jesus' mouth or in the water of the pool. Yet, when Lucas washed his eyes, they were opened, and for the first time in his life, he was able to see.

News of this healing caused quit a stir at the temple, especially because it was Sabbath. The healed blind man bore witness saying, "Since the world began it has been unheard of that anyone opened the eyes of one who was born blind. If this Man were not from God, He could do nothing." So they excommunicated Lucas.

When Jesus heard what had happened to Lucas, He hunted him down and asked, "Do you believe in the Son of Man?"

"Who is He, Lord, that I may believe in Him?" Lucas asked.

Jesus said to him, "You are looking at Him, and it is He who is talking to you."

Falling at Jesus' feet to worship, Lucas exclaimed, "Lord, I believe!"

Jesus' yearning heart was made glad. The miracle in Lucas' life was complete (based on John 9:1-41).

Today I invite you to accept Jesus as your Savior. Only Jesus can give sight to your blinded eyes. Only He can quench your thirsty soul and give you a joyous life. Jesus' heart is yearning for you to believe that He is able to save you completely, restore you fully, and fill you to overflowing with the blessings of salvation. God's Spirit lovingly entreats you, "Whosoever will, let him take the water of life freely." (Revelation 22:17 [KJV])

Chapter 26
ZEALOUS WORKER

"For unto us a Child is born, Unto us a Son is given; and the government will be upon His shoulder. And His name will be called Wonderful Counselor, Mighty God, Everlasting Father, Prince of Peace. Of the increase of His government and peace there will be no end. Upon the throne of David and over His kingdom, to order it and establish it with judgment and justice from that time forward, even forever. The zeal of the LORD of hosts will perform this." (Isaiah 9:6-7)

From Genesis to Revelation the Bible portrays how God is at work. Zealously the Creator works to accomplish His purposes for, in, and through man. God's thoughts are higher than mine, and His ways greater than I can comprehend. All of my attempts to describe His character or unveil His working are feeble and faulty. Yet I know that He doesn't do things half way, and He never gives up. His work turns out right and perfect. I believe God will move all heaven into operation to do His bidding. I stand in awe as I read how God zealously works for the salvation of His children. "I will meditate on all Your work, and talk of Your deeds. Your way, O God, is in the sanctuary. Who is so great a God as our God? You are the God who does wonders; You have declared Your strength among the peoples. You have with Your arm redeemed Your people, the sons of Jacob and Joseph." (Psalm 77:12-15)

In the history of Israel, we get a demonstration of God at work. Zealous for His cause God worked signs and wonders to deliver His people from bondage in Egypt. Plagues of frogs, flies, boils, hail, and more revealed that Israel's God was in charge. He opened the Red Sea so the multitude could cross safely on dry ground. He sent quail and manna from heaven to feed the multitudes. From a rock God caused water to flow forth, a stream sufficient for the people and their animals. He protected them from disease, vipers, and the sun. For forty years God led a people for whom He worked day and night.

When the Israelites reached Canaan, the first city to be conquered was Jericho. God instructed Joshua to have the men, led by priests blowing trumpets, to march around the city for seven days. On the seventh day, they were to make the circuit seven times, followed by a great shout. When they obeyed, God did the rest. The walls tumbled down, probably pushed by unseen angels. Talk about a job done with zeal!

During the conquest of Canaan, while fighting against the Amorites, Joshua prayed to God to make the sun stand still. "So the sun stood still and the moon stopped, till the people had revenge upon their enemies…And there has been no day like that, before it or after it, that the LORD heeded the voice of a man; for the LORD fought for Israel." (Joshua 10:12-14)

Another warrior, David, inquired of God, "Shall I go up against the Philistines? Will You deliver them into my hand?"

God told David, "I will deliver them into your hand." And He did. A while later the enemy came again. This time God gave David directions, "Circle around them and come upon them in front of the mulberry trees. And it shall be, when you hear a sound of marching in the tops of the mulberry trees, then you shall go out to battle, for God has gone out before you to strike the camp of the Philistines." The army was driven back and the fear of God was upon the nations (based on 1 Chronicles 14:10-16).

Another king who sought God's help against an enemy was King Hezekiah. Threatened by an Assyrian king named Sennacherib, who was reviling God's power, Hezekiah prayed, "O LORD our God, save us from his hand, that all the kingdoms of the earth may know that You are the LORD, You alone."

Through the prophet Isaiah, God assured Hezekiah, "Do not be afraid of the words which you have heard, with which the servants of the king of Assyria have blasphemed Me. Surely I will send a spirit upon him, and he shall hear a rumor and return to his own land; and I will cause him to fall by the sword in his own land. The zeal of the LORD of hosts will do this. He shall not come into this city, for I will defend this city to save it, for My own sake and for My servant David's sake." (based on Isaiah 37:6-35)

There's another fascinating account of God at work during Israel's history. The Syrian king went to war against the king of Israel, but his secret plans were not working out. Somehow the Israelite king always learned of his camping place. God was giving His prophet Elisha messages, which gave the king inside information. When the Syrian king learned who was responsible for leaking his strategy, he sent his army to surround the city of Dothan where Elisha and his servant were staying.

Fearfully, the servant exclaimed to Elisha, "Alas, my master! What shall we do?"

Elisha quietly replied, "Do not fear, for those who are with us are more than those who are with them." God had His own army of angels protecting His servant. "Show him, God," Elisha prayed. The Lord opened the young man's eyes, and he beheld the entire mountainside full of horses and chariots of fire.

The Syrian army planned to capture the prophet, but instead they were the ones captured. At Elisha's request God smote the entire army with blindness. Elisha himself led them inside Israel's capital city of Samaria and then asked God to open their eyes. "Shall I kill them?" Israel's king asked.

"No, feed them and give them water to drink," Elisha replied. So the king prepared a big feast for his enemies, and after the Syrians ate he sent them back home. The story ends, "so the bands of Syrian raiders came no more into the land of Israel" (based on 2 Kings 6:8-23). This story illustrates how God is zealously at work, not to destroy, but to win hearts for His kingdom. God always works for the good of His children and for His glory.

Much of Israel's history is sad. They not only failed to trust and obey God, they also turned their backs on Him and worshiped pagan idols. Yet, God loved them and continued working for their salvation. He sent them into captivity for seventy years as a punishment for their sins. Regarding the times of Israel's apostasy, the prophet Joel wrote, "Then the LORD will be zealous for His land, and pity His people." (Joel 2:18) God brought them back to Jerusalem as He'd promised. Even when people make wrong choices or fall into sin, God continues working with them. He seeks to heal, help, and redeem. That's why God sent His precious Son to this world.

While living on earth, Jesus faithfully did the works of God. His testimony to the Jews concerning His miracles and teachings was, "The Son can do nothing of Himself, but what He sees the Father do; for whatever He does, the Son also does in like manner. For the Father loves the Son, and shows Him all things that He Himself does; and He will show Him greater works than these, that you may marvel. For as the Father raises the dead and gives life to them, even so the Son gives life to whom He will. For the Father judges no one, but has committed all judgment to the Son, that all should honor the Son just as they honor the Father. He who does not honor the Son does not honor the Father who sent Him." (John 5:19-23) Just before going to the cross, Jesus told His disciple Philip, "He who has seen Me has seen the Father, so how can you say, 'Show us the Father?' Do you not believe that I am in the Father, and the Father in Me? The words that I speak to you I do not speak on My own authority; but the Father who dwells in Me does the works." (John 14:9, 10) Jesus told His Father, "I have glorified You on the earth. I have finished the work which You have given Me to do." (John 17:4)

God worked in and through His Son to give life to a dying world. Whether providing delicious grape juice for a wedding feast, healing a leper, hugging a child, or raising Lazarus from the dead, Jesus was doing the works of God. When Jesus took up the rope and commanded the scandalizing merchants to leave His Father's House, a scripture from Psalms came to His disciple's minds: "Zeal for Your house has eaten Me up." (John 2:17) Jesus is the most zealous worker ever to walk this earth, and His act is the greatest ever done. Everything Christ did was for man's salvation and God's glory.

The farthest reaching, all inclusive, most wonderful work of all time was when Jesus "bore our sins in His own body on the tree, that we, having died to sins, might live for righteousness—by whose stripes you were healed." (1 Peter 2:24) Jesus succeeded where Adam failed. (Romans 5:12-21) He perfectly obeyed God and never sinned. Jesus' perfect work He offers as a free gift to everyone. (1 John 3:5, 6) When you accept His package deal, God accepts you in His Son. Jesus assures us, "He who hears My word and believes in Him who sent Me has everlasting life, and shall not come into judgment, but has passed from death into life." (John 5:24) "There is therefore now no condemnation to those who are in Christ Jesus, who do not walk according to the flesh, but according to the Spirit. For the law of the Spirit of life in Christ Jesus has made me free from the law of sin and death." (Romans 8:1, 2)

The work of God's grace in us is the most amazing thing! God unites our weakness to His strength, our heart to His. He adopts us into His family! He takes out our stony, hardness of heart and gives us the mind of Jesus. God changes us on the inside to make us into precious jewels, His treasures. The cutting and polishing we may not like, but God has something beautiful in mind as He works to shape and shine us. We can be confident that He who has begun a good work in each of us will complete it until the day of Jesus Christ. (Philippians 1:6)

"For the grace of God that brings salvation has appeared to all men, teaching us that denying ungodliness and worldly lusts, we should live soberly, righteously, and godly in the present age, looking for the blessed hope and glorious appearing of our great God and Savior Jesus Christ, who gave Himself for us, that He might redeem us from every lawless deed and purify for Himself His own special people, zealous for good works." (Titus 2:11-14) God wants us to look to Him to do the work, for there is nothing we can do to be righteous or good. He is the One who redeems and purifies us. We can become enthusiastic about what He's doing and cooperate with His plan, but we cannot change ourselves or others. That's God's work.

Jesus gave Himself for us. He lives as our Savior. Today Jesus ministers in the heavenly sanctuary on our behalf. His work of mediation and intercession is for us. When we offer our prayers in Jesus' name, He presents them to the Father with His righteousness, and they ascend as fragrant incense to God. Further, Christ comes to us as the Comforter and the Teacher of righteousness, working in us and through us.

What should be our response to a God who is zealously at work to provide so much for His children? "Many, O LORD my God, are

Your wonderful works which You have done; and Your thoughts toward us cannot be recounted to You in order; if I would declare and speak of them, they are more than can be numbered." (Psalm 40:5)

I invite you today to accept Jesus' invitation, "Behold, I stand at the door and knock. If anyone hears My voice and opens the door, I will come in to him and dine with him, and he with Me." (Revelation 3:20) Jesus will bring the food! When Jesus is the Lord of our lives, He will transform our characters to reflect His own. We will be perfect in Christ. Alleluia! Amen!

Chapter 27

A PERSONAL GOD

"And this is life eternal, that they may know You, the only true God, and Jesus Christ whom You have sent." (John 17:3)

I suppose that if everyone wrote about God's character, the fullness of who He is could never be completely expressed. I have merely scratched the surface in attempting to share what God has revealed to me about His character of love. Friends, for all of eternity, the redeemed will be experiencing what God is like, and yet we will never comprehend the totality of our God. However, He wants us to know Him as He really is. His desire is to have a personal relationship with every individual. God says, "This is the covenant that I will make with the house of Israel after those days, says the Lord: I will put My law in their minds, and write it on their hearts; and I will be their God, and they shall be My people. No more shall every man teach his neighbor, and every man his brother, saying, 'Know the LORD,' for they all shall know Me, from the least of them to the greatest of them." (Jeremiah 31:33, 34)

God's law is an expression of His character. Both are unchangeable and everlasting. God promises to not only write His law—His character—in you, but to live and dwell in you by His Spirit. "If the Spirit of Him who raised Jesus from the dead dwells in you, He who raised Christ from the dead will also give life to your mortal bodies through His Spirit who dwells in you." (Romans 8:11) When you accept Jesus as your Savior, you have eternal life! "He who has the Son has life; he who does not have the Son of God does not have life." (1 John 5:12)

I appeal to you, seek Jesus. Ask Him to reveal the truth about God and His character to your heart. Seek to know God, not as an immortal, omniscient being alone, but as your Father who desires nothing but good for you. God is personal, and there is nothing He longs for more than to have an intimate relationship with you.

Let me leave you with these words from John, one of Jesus' beloved disciples. "No one has seen God at any time. If we love one another, God abides in us, and His love has been perfected in us. By this we know that we abide in Him, and He in us, because He has given us of His Spirit. And we have seen and testify that the Father has sent the Son as Savior of the world. Whoever confesses that Jesus is the Son of God, God abides in him, and he in God. And we have known and believed the love that God has for us. God is love, and he who abides in love abides in God, and God in him. Love has been perfected among us in this: that we may have boldness in the day of judgment; because as He is, so are we in this world. There is no fear in love; but perfect love casts out fear, because fear involves torment. But he who fears has not been made perfect in love. We love Him because He first loved us." (1 John 4:12-19)

If I could summarize God's character into one word, it would be this: LOVE. Personal love. Saving love. Everlasting love. God loves you! Won't you respond to His love?

We invite you to view the complete
selection of titles we publish at:

www.TEACHServices.com

or write or email us your praises,
reactions, or thoughts about this
or any other book we publish at:

TEACH Services, Inc.
P U B L I S H I N G
www.TEACHServices.com
P.O. Box 954
Ringgold, GA 30736

info@TEACHServices.com

TEACH Services, Inc., titles may be purchased in bulk for
educational, business, fund-raising, or sales promotional use.
For information, please e-mail

BulkSales@TEACHServices.com

Finally, if you are interested in seeing
your own book in print, please contact us at

publishing@teachservices.com

We would be happy to review your manuscript for free.

www.ingramcontent.com/pod-product-compliance
Lightning Source LLC
Chambersburg PA
CBHW031603110426
42742CB00036B/688